A FREE WEEKEND

Wine tasting

in California

Anne and David Yeadon

Camaro Publishing Co
LOS ANGELES–SAN FRANCISCO

Library of Congress Catalog Number 73-85632
ISBN   0−913290−05−X

CAMARO PUBLISHING COMPANY
LOS ANGELES, CALIFORNIA

For

John, Constance, Anne, Peter, Margery,
Roger, Cevin, Val, Gloria, Sandra, John,
Giles, Pam, Peter, Ted, and all offspring!

Preface

You don't need to be a wine connoisseur to enjoy good wines, of course, any more than you have to be an art expert in order to find pleasure in fine paintings and other works of art. Perhaps the hundreds of thousands of Americans who have traveled abroad have returned with a more adventurous spirit about food and drink. At any rate, the old mystique that once surrounded the subject of wine in this country is fast disappearing. No longer are wines thought to be reserved for the cognoscenti, the wealthy and sophisticated few who have mastered the mysterious and complicated business of wine etiquette. People are buying wines, serving them and drinking them without worrying about whether they are breaking the "rules." For, indeed, the only "rule" about wine is that it ought to be selected and consumed with the attention, respect and appreciation that almost surely went into its making.

Americans can rightfully be proud of their native wines, particularly those made in California. Today, fine California wines receive the worldwide recognition they have so long deserved. Domestic labels are no longer assumed to be somehow "inferior" to imported offerings; in fact, the best of the U. S.—made wines are highly prized and sought after in the traditional wine-producing areas of Europe. I am sure that 50 years from now, bottles of vintage Cabernet Sauvignon, Zinfandel and other domestic varietals will occupy privileged niches in wine shops and private collections both here and abroad.

How can you get the maximum amount of pleasure from wine? How can you choose the wines you like best from the bewildering variety of types and brands available to most Californians? Knowledge of wines comes only from tasting them. In recent years, more and more wineries have opened tasting rooms and invited the public to sample their wares—a delightful practice which has helped remove much of the mystery concerning wine.

This book opens the way to learning about and appreciating the wines of California. In the pages that follow, you'll find tantalizing glimpses of the places where they can be tasted and purchased, of the procedures used in producing them and of the dedicated and enthusiastic people who make them—along with practical information to guide you in conducting your own exploration. The rest is up to you.

And now, "fill the glass if it is empty, and empty the glass if it is full."

Pancho L. Alliati

Palos Verdes Peninsula

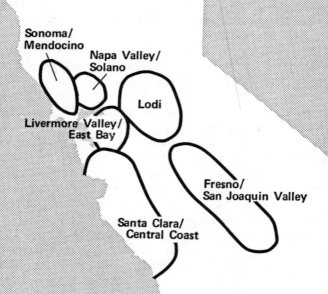

Sonoma/
Mendocino

Napa Valley/
Solano

Lodi

Livermore Valley/
East Bay

Fresno/
San Joaquin Valley

Santa Clara/
Central Coast

Cucamonga/
Los Angeles

*California
Wine Regions*

Contents

Wine Tasting Is Fun!

A weekend in the Wine Country—what better way to enjoy fine scenery, fresh air and the generous bounties of nature to be found in a single glass of fine Cabernet Sauvignon?

Depending on the season, the region and the winery itself, visitor facilities vary enormously. At one of the smaller, family-owned establishments, a guest may find himself sipping wines in a cellar under the house or in a corner of the aging room, as the smell of cooking wafts in from a nearby kitchen. Alternatively, at a larger winery, tourists may be met by the sounds of piped music and an exotically costumed tour guide who will skip and dance them through a timed-to-the-minute tour, answering intelligent questions with the speed and ambiguity of a third-term political incumbent.

These are extreme examples, however; most tasting rooms are pleasant appendages to the main wineries, where visitors are made to feel welcome and respected. The hosts, generally well-versed in wine lore, will welcome questions and opinions and eagerly offer thorough samplings of their wineries' products. (A warning: people who are primarily interested in a free hangover will find that most hosts are well trained in the art of polite rejection!)

Of course, getting stuck in a summer Sunday traffic snarl while negotiating the narrow wine-valley roads, only to end up standing in line at a tasting-room bar for a thimbleful of warm Riesling, is not an ideal introduction to this form of weekend recreation.

The best time to visit the Wine Country is in the fall. Although there is no guarantee even then of traffic-free roads, at least there will be a little action at the normally tranquil wineries. Autumn is the harvesting and crushing season, and watching the huge stemmer-and-crusher machines at work can lead to an understanding of and fascination for the wonderful and subtle process of wine making. Or, for a more relaxed guided stroll around the wineries, unharassed by scores of tourists, plan a trip during the winter months, when makers have more time to discuss their art and tastings are more leisurely and infor-mative. If it is raining outside, the tasting rooms will seem all the more appealing. Weekdays are the best times to avoid crowds.

In this book we have attempted to provide the interested layman with an "information kit" for a tour of the wineries. We have assumed that our readers know the basics of wines, and so have avoided giving protracted lectures on wine history, wine cliches and wine myths.

We have also assumed that readers are pri-marily interested in those wineries which can be visited without prior appointment. Thus, most of the book discusses establishments that offer tours and tastings on a daily basis throughout the year.

Wineries that provide tastings or tours by appointment only are listed at the back of the book, along with a few interesting newcomers.

We have also tried, in a straightforward manner, to provide the reader with a broad overview of the wine industry in California as it exists today, along with some useful pieces of information (including a glossary of wine terms) which will increase his understanding and enjoyment of this fascinating world.

Finally, to help remove some of the mystique which surrounds wines and wine appreciation generally, we have suggested a simple procedure for wine tasting and evaluation. More complex systems, such as those used by professional wine tasters, exist; however, these tend to be unnecessarily confusing to the uninitiated. We hope that the charts at the back of the book will enable the interested visitor to the wine country to maintain a record of his samplings and experience more knowledgeable and valuable tasting sessions. The delights of wine are infinite, as are the pleasures of exploring California's wine country and its scores of fascinating wineries. *Skol.*

Anne & David Yeadon

A Few Useful Notes

THE CALIFORNIA WINE INDUSTRY—
A BRIEF OVERVIEW

In the last few years California wines have achieved an all-time record popularity throughout the United States, and won new respect in Europe. Over 70 percent of all wines consumed in this country are produced in California. Unfortunately, production—particularly of the premium varietal wines—cannot keep pace with demand, which has resulted in higher wine prices. Bottles of vintage Cabernet Sauvignon produced and bottled at some of California's finer wineries can occasionally be found retailing at between $8 and $15—considerably more than many imported European vintages.

No one can estimate accurately how rapidly this demand will increase or how consistently it will continue. However, a few years ago wine maker Ernest Gallo projected that the total consumption of wine in the U.S. would amount to some 1.3 billion gallons by 1994, compared with a 1970 total of some 270 million gallons.

The Gallos have always been optimists, but they also have an impressive ability to predict and provide for important trends.

Wines are now big business in the U.S. The small family wineries are rapidly becoming another romantic memory. Huge conglomerates are spreading their tentacles along the wine valleys; inflated prices are being paid for the products of low-production California wineries with "names." Already such companies as Heublein, National Distillers, Nestle, Pillsbury and Seagram own many of the major wineries in the premium areas; if the trend continues unchecked, it is possible that within a few years a large proportion of California wine production will be controlled from the clinical boardrooms of a handful of mammoth companies. Fortunately, there are other, more promising developments. In the last three years a number of exclusive, limited-production (25,000 to 50,000 gallons annually) wineries have been established. Although they tend to appeal to elitist wine consumers, they nevertheless reflect an increasing degree of appreciation of high-quality California wines.

The wine revolution, which began after Prohibition but gained real momentum in the 1960s, has generated a host of new and fascinating developments in the science of wine—enology. The University of California at Davis has made many notable contributions to the industry in the form of new grape varieties (Ruby Cabernet, Emerald Riesling, Ruby Red, etc.) and has developed a method for mechanical harvesting and crushing-in-the-field in association with the Mirassou winery. At the other end of the scale, enthusiastic individuals, such as F. Justin Miller, have conceived new approaches

14

to wine production. Although Miller's unique process for producing instant champagne is still ignored by the major wine producers, his influence may ultimately be felt throughout the industry.

It would be futile to try to produce an accurate world picture of how the California wine industry will look in the future. But a journey through the Napa and Sonoma valleys, where impressive ultra-contemporary projects by Sterling, Souverain, and other producers are currently being developed, should be enough to show that the industry in California is no longer adolescent in nature. Maturity may not be the right word, but there can be no doubt that wines are now big business and that they will be developed with all the vigor and dynamism that has characterized American enterprise for the last 150 years. We hope that amidst all the tumult of an industry in the process of frantic expansion, the subtle secrets of fine wine making will not be lost.

CALIFORNIA WINES

California wines are divided into two distinct categories: generic and varietal. Generic wines are those named after European wine production areas: e.g., burgundy, moselle, sauterne, chablis and rhine; or those with such general titles as vin rosé, vin blanc and chianti. Such wines contain blends of numerous grape types, and may vary significantly in content from winery to winery.

Varietal wines, on the other hand, must contain at least 51 percent of the grape variety named on the label. Such titles as Pinot Noir, Cabernet Sauvignon and Gewürztraminer are indicative of the primary grape contained in the bottle. Unfortunately, little control is exercised over the remaining 49 percent of

the wine; and since only a few select wineries produce varietals containing 100 percent of the named
grape, varietals vary enormously in content.

Following are brief descriptions of some of
California's better-known premium or varietal wines.

RED WINES

Barbera (bar-bear´-ah) A grape from Northern Italy,
it normally possesses a rich, fruity aroma, but tends
to be tart unless well aged.

Cabernet Sauvignon (ka-bear-nay´ so-vee-nyon´)
Often regarded as the king of California wines,
Cabernet Sauvignon is the prime varietal of the
famed Bordeaux wines. A young Cabernet tends
to be tart and unpleasantly rough; in its mature state
the wine is deep-colored and full-bodied, often pos-
sessing great subtlety.

Gamay or Gamay Beaujolais (gah-may´ bo-zho-lay´)
There is still confusion as to which of these grapes
is the true Beaujolais wine grape. Nevertheless,
both types produce wine which is light and fruity.

Petite Sirah (puh-teet´ Syr-ah´) Until recently this
grape was normally used as a blending wine, but
some notable varietals have been produced which
are rich and ample-bodied.

Pinot Noir (pee-no´ nwor) The great black grape
used in the famous Burgundy wines of France.
The Pinot Noir wines of California still vary
enormously in quality, though a few rich, full-
bodied vintages have been achieved. In addition,
many California wine makers feel that a certain
degree of lightness is desirable in a California Pinot
Noir. These wine makers therefore produce Pinot
Noirs on their own merits, not as duplicates of
those from Burgundy.

Ruby Cabernet (roo´-bee ka-bear-nay´) A grape developed by the University of California at Davis, it possesses some of the characteristics of a Cabernet Sauvignon, although less pronounced.

Pinot St. George (pee-no´ sein zhorge) A fruity, aromatic wine, delicate to the taste, produced almost exclusively in the Napa Valley.

Zinfandel (zin´-fan-dell) Zinfandel is one of the most widely planted wine grapes in California, and the quality of its wine varies enormously. At its best it is a zesty wine, fruity and aromatic, and normally reasonably priced.

WHITE WINES

Chenin Blanc (she-ne´ blon) One of the primary grapes of the Loire Valley in France, it produces a light, fruity wine and is normally medium-dry.

Emerald Riesling (rees ling) Another grape developed by the University of California at Davis. The wine is fresh and tart.

French Colombard A somewhat neutral dry wine appearing more often as a generic.

Gewürztraminer (ge-wurtz-trah-me´-ner) This grape produces some of the best rhine-type wines in the state—spicy, light-bodied and fragrant.

Green Hungarian Although normally used as a blending wine, some exceptionally crisp, dry varietals have been produced recently in the Northern California wine areas. Some wineries have also produced a semisweet version of this wine.

Grey Riesling A somewhat neutral wine of a mild spicy character.

Johannisberg Riesling The premier grape of the rhine

and moselle regions. The wine has a rich, fragrant flavor but varies widely in dryness.

Pinot Blanc (pee-no' blon) A distinctive wine, keen in aroma and flavor but occasionally overacidic.

Pinot Chardonnay or Chardonnay (pee-no' shar'-doe-nay) This delicate grape produces the famous white Burgundies and Chablis of France. One of the true "flinty" wines, full-bodied, fragrant and smooth.

Sauvignon Blanc (so-vee-nyon' blon) The Graves and Sauternes of the Bordeaux region are produced from this noble grape. The wine is distinctively aromatic and unusually full-bodied.

Sauvignon Vert (so-vee-nyon' vair) Normally used for blending purposes, this grape produces a dry wine with a noticeable Muscat flavor.

Semillon (say-me-yon) Often used in conjunction with Sauvignon Blanc to produce a wide variety of California sauternes. As a varietal it has rich flavor and a distinct flowerlike aroma. It varies considerably in degree of sweetness.

Sylvaner (sill-vahn'-er) This grape produces a somewhat neutral wine with a pleasantly distinct aroma.

ROSES

Grenache Rosé (gre-nash' ro-zay') This grape produces some of the finest rosé wine in California, with varying degrees of sweetness.

Most other rosés are derived from Gamay, Grignolino, Cabernet Sauvignon and Zinfandel grapes.

MISCELLANEOUS FACTS

Or How to Become an Instant Wine Expert!

- Invite your guests to sample your selected

dinner wine prior to the meal. This will increase their enjoyment of it during the meal.

- If your local liquor store displays all its wines in an upright position, buy your wines somewhere else.
- During wine tastings sponsored by the Wine Institute from 1956–1958, California wines compared exceptionally well with their European counterparts—much to the surprise of many French vintners!
- It takes 14,000 grapes to produce a gallon of dessert wine and 7,000 for a gallon of table wine.
- Rosés are generally short-life wines. Beware of brown discoloration.
- Always open a red dinner wine an hour or so before the meal to allow it to "breathe" (half an hour maximum for white wines).
- A fifth of table wine will normally be adequate for three or four people.
- Do not reject screw-capped wines out of hand. The use of cork is normally only essential for some premium wines likely to undergo a considerable period of bottle-aging.
- Avoid restaurants with one-winery wine lists. It's normally a sign of ignorance or indifference to wines on the part of the management.
- Do not be overawed by the mention of medals and awards on wine labels. Almost every winery has a drawerful.
- If you ever need to justify the physiological benefit of wine, read Dr. Salvatore Lucia's book *Wine as Food and Medicine* (Blakiston Inc., 1954), and also *Wine and Your Well-being*, by the same author, available from the Wine Advisory Board and in many book stores.

- Expand your vocabulary of wine-related adjectives. Expressions such as *bold, robust, flinty, fresh, crisp, earthy, heavy, acidy, chewy, rough, woody, berrylike, clean, tart, weedy* and *sulfurous* form a precise language for comparison and communication.
- Don't be overawed by impressive-looking European wine labels. Many inferior brands and vintages are imported into the U.S.
- We have it on good authority that Italian wines no longer contain bulls' blood.

FOR YOUR FURTHER READING ENJOYMENT

Many fine books have been published about California wines. We found the following both useful and enjoyable:

The Commonsense Book of Wine, by Leon D. Adams. David McKay Co., New York, 1968. In this none-too-delicate blast at wine snobs who have wrapped wines and wine making in a mantle of mystique and exclusiveness Mr. Adams tears away the murky shrouds and reveals, to the unitiated, the fascinating pleasures to be derived from a basic knowledge and understanding of wines.

Wine: An Introduction for Americans, by M.A. Amerine and V.L. Singleton. University of California Press, Berkeley, 1965. This is an excellent publication for the serious student of wines. The initial chapters on the chemistry of wine making are particularly fascinating. The wines and wine regions of the world are thoroughly discussed, and there is a final section on wine appreciation, evaluation and service.

Guide to California Wines, by John Melville (third edition revised by Jefferson Morgan). Nourse

Publishing Co., San Carlos, California, 1968. A comprehensive and authoritative guide to the wines and wineries of California, including histories of the wineries and the wines produced.

Adventures in the Wine Country, by Jefferson Morgan. Chronicle Books, San Francisco, 1971. A fresh, amusing book, similar in content to Melville's book, but lighter in tone and illustrated with photographs of the wine country.

The Wine Bibber's Bible, by James Norwood Pratt. 101 Productions, San Francisco, 1971. An interesting collection of essays on wine tasting, wine making and wine buying, illustrated by Sara Raffetto's delicate drawings.

The Fine Wines of California, by Hurst Hannum and Robert S. Blumberg. Doubleday & Co., New York, 1971. A courageous effort by two young wine experts to evaluate over 400 wines from more than 40 California wineries. The authors also discuss wine in general, wine types, wine appreciation and the California wine industry.

In addition to these publications, the Wine Institute and Wine Advisory Board (both located at 717 Market St., San Francisco 94103) have produced a number of useful booklets on California wines. These are available free of charge at most wineries and from the Wine Institute, and are fine examples of simple, descriptive writing. The Wine Advisory Board also offers a wine study course, free on application. Write to them for details.

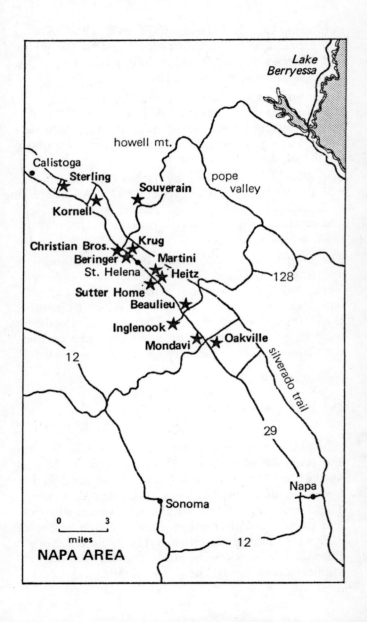

Lake Berryessa

howell mt.

Calistoga

Sterling

pope valley

Souverain

Kornell

Krug

Christian Bros.

Beringer

St. Helena

Martini

Heitz

Sutter Home

Beaulieu

128

Inglenook

Mondavi

Oakville

silverado trail

12

29

Sonoma

Napa

12

0   3

miles

NAPA AREA

Napa Valley / Solano Region

The name Napa is referred to with awe and respect by wine lovers the world over. Even the French are now beginning to take an active interest in the Napa Valley's wineries, particularly those small establishments specializing in limited productions of prime varietals.

The microclimatic characteristics of the Napa Valley are eminently suitable for the cultivation of the finest grape stocks. The vineyards around St. Helena, the hub of the prime growing area, are rich in Cabernet Sauvignon, Pinot Noir, Gewürztraminer and Semillon grapes, and land values in 1973 reached an all-time high of around $10,000 an acre—an interesting contrast to the situation a little over a hundred years ago, when average values were about $100 an acre.

The Napa Valley wineries form a cohesive lobby that wields an amazing amount of power over the small city councils in the area. Occasionally there are conflicts of interest, particularly when tax-conscious councilmen struggle to allocate land for urban development in prime grape-growing areas. But generally the relationship is amicable; both the cities and wineries recognize that Napa wines are currently enjoying an unprecedented degree of national and world prominence, and that every effort must be made to ensure continuous and prosperous growth of the valley's economy. The recent passage in the state legislature of the Williamson Act has resulted in the establishment of an agriculture preserve in the Napa Valley which grape growers hope will curtail urban development outside the presently established city boundaries.

Of course, the tourist knows nothing of this. He sees the rich vineyards and the magnificent old winery buildings; he tastes some of the world's finest wines—and that's how it should be.

Beaulieu

Beaulieu in French means "beautiful place," but to many people the Beaulieu Vineyard is known as simply "BV." It was founded in 1900 by Georges de Latour, who had come to California in his mid-twenties. After a whirl in the Gold Rush, he became interested in chemistry. Under the gentle pressure of Archbishop Riordan, Latour was encouraged to buy land and enter the wine making business in order to help meet the demands for sacramental wine. He founded his winery in the Napa Valley and spent the following years importing vines from Europe. Latour is said to have been the first vintner to introduce Cabernet Sauvignon to this part of the country.

In 1937, when the winery had become a bulk operation, Latour employed as production manager Andre Tchelistcheff, who only recently retired after 36 years at Beaulieu. After Latour died in 1940, his wife managed the winery until her death in 1951, after which ownership passed to his daughter and son-in-law, Madame and the Marquis de Pins. In 1969 Beaulieu became one of the wine companies owned by Heublein Inc. Today, the traditions of classical wine making established by Latour and his successors are being continued by Dr. Richard C. Peterson, who works closely with the Beaulieu tasting panel.

The tours at Beaulieu are interesting and informative. The new redwood tanks that are recent additions were apparently made on the premises. Most of the wine is aged in 50-gallon oak casks. The small bottling plant produces approximately 1,400 cases of wine a day. The bottles are then stored for two or three months before leaving the plant. (If you notice that some bottles are sealed with screw caps, instead of corks, they're meant for the airlines or for sacramental purposes—to be consumed within a year.) Although the winery makes its own *brut* champagne by the old method of bottle fermentation *(methode champenoise)* these facilities are in a separate location and not open to the public.

Tasting may be enjoyed before or after the tour in the spacious modern stone and wood room. Wine is poured

out of the sight of guests—
an unfortunate practice,
since the sampler does not
always see the bottle. Hope-
fully, this policy will change
when the new two-level
visitor center and tasting
facilities (now under construction) are completed.

The labels on the
Beaulieu bottles are especially informative, and
almost all its wines are
vintaged. Cabernet Sauvi-
gnon and Gamay Beaujolais
are just two wines from
an extensive selection of
which the winery is exceptionally proud.

*1960 St. Helena Highway
(Highway 29), Rutherford;
(707) 963-3617; daily
10 - 4; guided tours.*

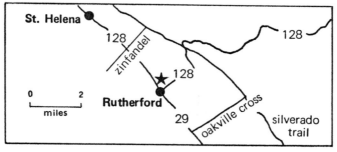

Beringer

The elegant Rhine House at the Beringer Brothers winery is one of the most impressive wine-tasting and guest-reception centers in California. Stained-glass windows, beautiful chandeliers and hostesses in long gowns are just a few of the highlights of this 17-room mansion, which was built in 1883 by Frederick and Jacob Beringer as a replica of the home they had left behind in Germany. In 1971 the family sold the winery to the Nestlé Company with the understanding that Nestlé would continue the Beringer tradition.

The cellars, which were hacked out of solid limestone in 1876, are the main attraction of the short but quite interesting tour. The maze of tunnels, used today as the main aging area, extends over 1,000 feet and maintains a constant temperature of approximately 58 degrees. American white oak barrels, coopered in Spain, have recently been added to Beringer's cellars to supplement the oak storage capacity of the 50 to 100-year-old oak casks.

Barenblut (translated "blood of the bear") is a secret blend of three grape varieties and is made only by Beringer Brothers. Fume Blanc (produced by only one other winery in the valley), Zinfandel, Johannisberg Riesling, Cabernet Sauvignon and Gamay Rosé represent samples of the winery's fine selection.

2000 Main Street, Los Hermanos Vineyards, St. Helena; (707) 963-7115; daily 9:30 - 4; guided tours.

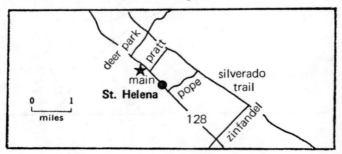

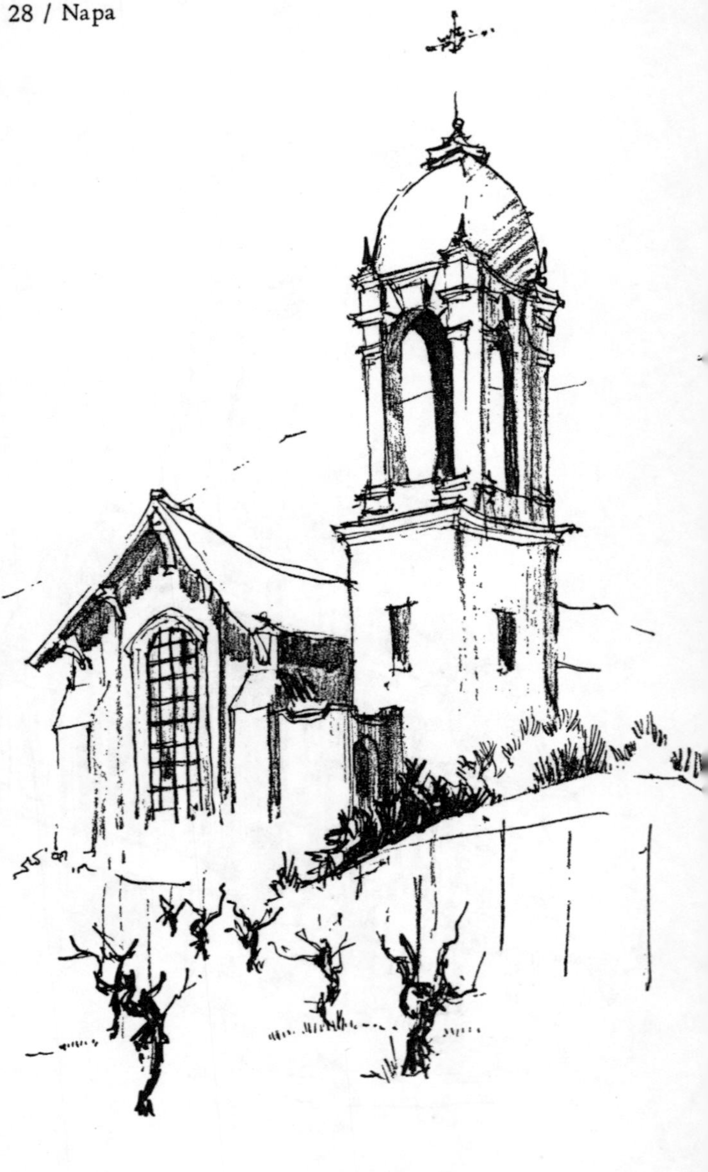

The Christian Brothers

The 300-year-old teaching order of the Roman Catholic Church known as The Brothers of the Christian Schools or, more familiarly, The Christian Brothers, was founded in Rheims, France in 1680 by St. Jean Baptiste de la Salle. The Brothers settled in California in 1868, and in 1879 planted vines for the purpose of producing sacramental wines. As time went by they began selling their surplus wines on a commercial basis, and today their wines are found throughout the U.S.

There are two Christian Brothers wineries in the Napa area open to the public for tasting and tours. The first, Mont LaSalle, is an old stone winery built in 1903 by Theodore Gier, the former owner of the estate. The training school (novitiate) overlooks the winery and the adjoining vineyards. A tour of this winery is apt to be more enjoyable than a visit to the Brothers' St. Helena Wine and Champagne Cellars, built by William Bowers Bourn in 1889, where tours are more hurried and questions are not always answered adequately. Construction of a multimillion-dollar complex, including new crushing, fermenting and warehouse areas, is due to begin shortly on the south edge of St. Helena.

Mont La Salle, 4411 Redwood Road, Napa; (707) 226-5566; Main Street, St. Helena; (707) 963-2719; daily 10 - 4:30; guided tours.

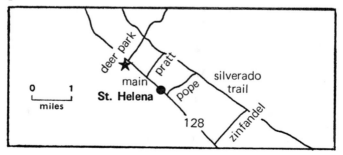

Heitz

Joe Heitz's philosophy is to create "fine wines of out-standing quality, even though the price may be high." Prices at his Heitz wine cellars are on the high side, but it is generally accepted that Heitz has a reputation to match. His 1971 Johannisberg Riesling, 1970 Pinot Blanc Lyncrest and 1970 Pinot Blanc McCrea are considered to be particularly outstanding. In contrast to other huge, impressive wineries of the Napa Valley, the Heitz tasting room sits quietly alone on the St. Helena Highway. If you wish to visit the actual winery, in a beautiful setting up in the hills east of St. Helena, you must make an appointment.

Joe Heitz had at one time seriously considered becoming a veterinarian. Obviously, something happened along the way to make him change his mind. After graduating in viticulture and enology from the University of California at Davis, he worked for a while with Gallo and then Beaulieu. He later taught at Fresno State, where he pioneered the enology department. In 1961 Heitz decided to take the plunge and buy his own winery.

Rollie, Joe's youngest son, has a corner of the tasting room to display his aged vinegar, packaged bay leaves, mushrooms and pre-Prohibition champagne bottles. The regular newsletter produced by Joe and his wife, Alice, brings clients up to date on new wines and explains each one individually. It's a thoughtful service.

Winery: 500 Taplin Road, St. Helena; Tasting room: 436 St. Helena Highway, St. Helena; (707) 963-3542; daily 11 - 5; tours by appointment.

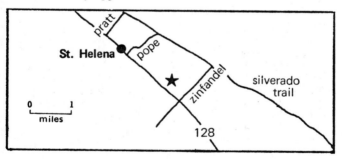

Inglenook

In 1879 a wealthy Finnish seafarer, Captain Gustave Niebaum, purchased land in the Napa Valley and designed and built Inglenook's present ivy-clad stone wine cellar, using Chinese labor to quarry rock from the nearby hills. Massive walls of hewn stone and arched cellars were constructed to provide a natural environment where wines could be aged at a constant temperature throughout the year. Within ten years of the founding of his winery, Niebaum's wines received distinguished recognition at the Paris Exposition of 1889.

In 1968 Inglenook was purchased by Heublein, but little seems to have changed since Niebaum's days. His old sample room (on sight as you enter the cellars), is designed as a ship's wardroom and displays furniture of hand-carved oak from the Black Forest in Germany, and the decorated ceiling was brought in its entirety from the Rhineland.

The tours of the winery are not particularly outstanding, although the management is now giving some thought to

changing them. Because crushing and fermenting are performed at another Inglenook facility down the road, the visitor sees little other than the old tasting room and the aging cellars.

Inglenook has an extensive selection of table and dessert wines. Most of these are available for tasting, with the exception of Cabernet. All its wines are vintaged except the Navalle wines, a relatively new lower-cost wine.

Highway 29 on private road, Rutherford; (707) 963-7182; daily, Nov. - Apr., 10 - 4; May - Oct. 9 - 5; guided tours.

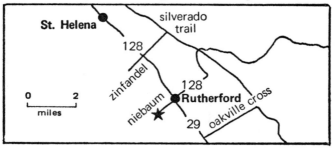

Kornell

Hanns Kornell fled Germany during the Hitler regime in 1939 and arrived in the U.S. without money. For a number of years he worked at whatever and wherever he could. But gradually he found his way into the champagne business. Kornell is a master of the traditional method of champagne making *(champenoise)* introduced to him by members of his family, who were wine and champagne makers in Germany. His skills began to develop when he worked for the Fountaingrove winery in Santa Rosa (see Martini & Prati), the Gibson Wine Co. and, later, the American Wine Co. in St. Louis Missouri.

In 1952 he leased a winery in Sonoma, the Sonoma Wine Company, and rechristened it the Hanns Kornell Cellars. In 1958 he bought a winery on Larkmead Lane in the Napa Valley—the present Hanns Kornell Champagne Cellars in St. Helena.

During a time of 20th-century mechanization, the Hanns Kornell Cellars remains one of the few wineries which concentrate on the traditional methods of making champagne. All its champagnes are sold in the same bottle in which they are produced. Prior to bottling, individual wines are blended together and sugar and yeast are added. The wine is then bottled and stacked for approximately two years. During this time, as the wine is undergoing a second fermentation, the released carbon dioxide introduces the sparkle and bubbles characteristic of champagne. The bottles are then placed in an upside-down position for a period of eight to ten weeks. At this point man's patience is introduced: each bottle is turned by hand, a quarter-turn each day (notice the white mark on the "well" of the bottle which acts as a memory guide). As a result of this regular rotation, the sediment left after the fermentation works its way down to the neck of the bottle. The bottle neck is then placed into a freezing solution. When the bottle cap is removed, the internal pressure forces out the frozen sediment. This process is known as disgorging. The bottle is then topped up with champagne from a reservoir bottle.

Prior to sealing, a carefully regulated amount of blended cane sugar, wine and brandy is added. (This is the *dosage* that governs the ultimate sweetness of the champagne.) The bottle is then corked and stored for three or four months prior to distribution.

The entire process is explained during the tour of the cellars and, of course, tasting is available in the tiny reception room. Hanns Kornell considers all his champagnes to be outstanding, but he is particularly proud of his Sehr Trocken—a very dry champagne introduced in 1972 during his 20th year as a champagne maker.

Larkmead Lane, just north of St. Helena; (707) 963-2334; daily 10 - 5; guided tours.

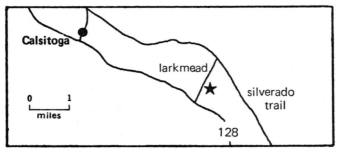

Charles Krug (C. Mondavi & Sons)

Before touring the Charles Krug Winery, take a look at the cider press that holds the visitors' registration book. This was used by Charles Krug back in the old days, prior to his founding the Krug Ranch winery in 1861. From the press, Krug made 1,200 gallons of wine—the first wine in the valley to be made by modern methods. He worked closely with Agoston Haraszthy (see Buena Vista) and General Mariano Vallejo (a well-known wine pioneer), but quickly became an established figure in his own right. After Krug died in 1892, his two daughters sold the ranch to friends, the Moffitt family, who used it as their private home.

In 1943 the ranch was sold again to an Italian family that had begun to make its presence felt in the California wine industry: Cesare Mondavi and his two sons, Robert and Peter. Since the death of Cesare in 1959, the winery has remained in the family, although Robert recently launched out on his own (see Mondavi winery).

The tour itself is interesting and informative. At its conclusion, three wines are presented for tasting. We sampled the Dry Semillon, a vin rosé (made from Gamay and Grenache grapes) and Chenin Blanc, which is one of the winery's most popular varietals. Its wine is bottled under two labels: Charles Krug (premium wines) and C. K. Mondavi (primarily shipped to restaurants).

The famous August Moon Concerts are held here during the summer, with tastings offered during intermissions. For information, write to August Moon Concerts, P. O. Box 535, Napa, California 94558.

Main Street, north St. Helena; (707) 963-2761; daily 10 - 4; guided tours.

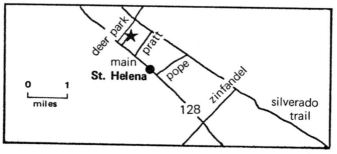

Louis M. Martini

Louis Martini's interest in wine dates back to 1906 (the year of the great San Francisco earthquake), when he left San Francisco and his father's fish and clam business and returned to Italy to study wine making. After a short time he returned to California, where he worked for several California wine makers before he eventually built his own winery in the San Joaquin Valley, specializing in the production of sweet wines and brandy. His dream, however, was to create wines of premium quality, and for this reason he ultimately chose to settle in the Napa Valley in 1934.

In addition to the more usual varietals, Martini produces Gewürztraminer and Folle Blanche. His generics include claret, chianti, chablis, dry sauternes and burgundy. A limited supply of his Private Reserve and Special Selection labels are sold only at the winery: 1964 and 1966 Cabernet Sauvignon, 1965 and 1966 Pinot Noir, 1968 Pinot Chardonnay and 1969 Johannisberg Riesling are presently available. All his varietals are vintage-dated.

Tours are available upon request, but are not a required passport to tasting.

Highway 128, south of St. Helena; (707) 963-2736; daily 10 - 4; guided tours on request.

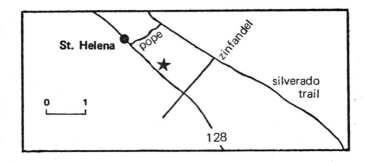

Robert Mondavi

Robert Mondavi's Mission-style winery was established in 1966. Designed by Cliff May, the winery is one of the most sophisticated in the valley today.

In 1966 Robert broke away from the Krug winery, now owned by the Mondavi family, and with his son, Michael, entered a partnership with the Rainer Brewing Company of Seattle. Their aim was to produce high-quality wines of distinctive character. Their current reputation would suggest that they are succeeding admirably.

The tour at the Robert Mondavi Winery begins with a dissertation on the growth of vines and grapes. Visitors are then led through an immaculate winery equipped with the most expensive and up-to-date wine-producing machinery in California: a $100,000 vacuum filter that processes one ton of bulk wine in three minutes (paid for in one crushing season by filtering commissions from other wineries), a French-made machine that separates juice from skins for the production of white wine, a German centrifuge machine that cleans the juice prior to fermentation, a vast array of

stainless steel tanks, and row upon row of Limousin and Yugoslavian oak barrels used for aging the wines. Needless to say, Mondavi's impressive equipment is the envy of many of the Napa wineries.

Three wines are usually offered at the tasting room, after the tour. These may include, Johannisberg Riesling, Fume Blanc, Chardonnay, Gamay Rosé, Gamay Pinot Noir or Chenin Blanc.

Highway 29, north of Oakville; (707) 963-7156; daily 10 - 4:30; guided tours.

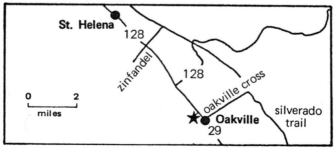

Oakville

A relative newcomer to the Napa Valley wineries is Oakville Vineyards. Oakville is the first winery and producing vineyard to be financed a public limited partnership, and W. E. van Löben Sels serves as the general partner. A recent purchase of 110 acres of producing vineyards by a related corporation from the Inglenook Estate promises to result in a significant increase in its wine production.

Although tours are only offered by appointment at this winery, its tasting room displays a wide variety of wine-related gifts and a full range of Oakville wines for sampling. Their varietals contain a full 100 percent of the named label-grape, in contrast to the 51 percent minimum required by law. Napa Gamay Rosé, Zinfandel, Chenin Blanc 1971, Sauvignon Blanc 1971 Reserve and red and white house wines, are just a few of the winery's selections. All Oakville wine is sold under the Oakville and van Löben Sels labels.

Oakville Cross Road at State Highway 29, Oakville;
(707) 944-2455; daily 10 - 4:30; tours by appointment only.

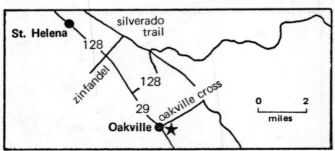

Souverain

Thirty years ago a man by the name of J. Leland Stewart bought a chicken ranch on the slopes of Howell Mountain in the Sonoma Valley, on which he found a small winery building dating back to 1870. Fascinated by wine making, he began producing wines. Stewart's Souverain Cellars was the first winery in California to produce Green Hungarian as a varietal, but his initial releases were Johannisberg Riesling and Zinfandel.

In 1970, due to ill health in the family, Lee Stewart retired and sold the winery to a corporation, but continues to play a significant role in the business. A new complex resembling a contemporary version of a Dutch barn has recently been constructed in a magnificent location overlooking the Napa Valley.

Another new winery, Ville Fontaine near Geyserville, is scheduled to be opened in late 1973. Ville Fontaine will be a more visitor-oriented facility, with tour guides, five tasting rooms and a high-quality restaurant—a much-needed addition in the area. Two massive towers, with shapes reminiscent of the hop kilns that once were a familiar sight throughout the Sonoma area, and a large fountain will serve as landmarks for the Ville Fontaine complex.

Intersection 128 at Silverado Trail, Souverain Road, Rutherford; (707) 963-2759; daily 8:30 - 4:30; guided tours weekdays 10:30 to 2:30; weekends 10 - 4:30.

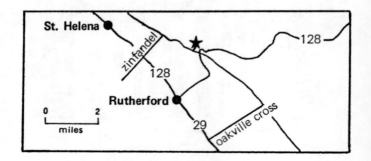

Sterling

This winery, a magnificent new structure of Mediterranean design on a hilltop site, opened in the summer of 1973.
It is managed by two families, the Newtons and the Stones. The owners had purchased the land in 1964 and, since there were no existing vineyards, planted all new stock.

The winery places an unusually heavy emphasis on visitor facilities. An aerial tramway ($2 fee) provides transportation for visitors to the tour and tasting facilities on the top of the hill. There 18th-century bells brought from England will peal a resounding welcome at regular intervals. Guests will be guided in a leisurely, take-your-own-time fashion through galleries overlooking the working areas, and audio and visual aids will augment the tours. Providing a relaxing and informal, yet educational, experience for visitors appears to be one of the prime goals of the infant corporation.

Sterling Vineyards does not plan to produce any generics. The winery now has ready for release six prime varietal wines: Cabernet Sauvignon, Zinfandel, Blanc de Sauvignon, Chenin Blanc and Gewürztraminer, plus an exceptional Pinot Chardonnay.

Sterling wines are sold exclusively at the winery, so a visit there for their specially priced wines is definitely in order.

1111 Dunaweal Lane, Calistoga; (707) 942-6257; daily 11 - 6; self-guided tours 10:30 - 5.

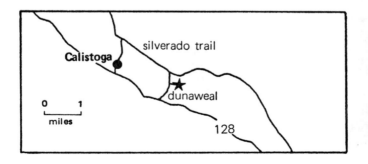

Sutter Home

A winery in the Napa Valley which specializes in one wine is a rarity. But the Trinchero family intends to devote 80 percent of its production to one of California's most popular varietals, Zinfandel. The tasting room, part of which dates back to 1874, currently offers a range of table and dessert wines; but by 1974 the Trincheros hope to produce a more specialized list, consisting of no more than five wines.

The history of the Sutter Home Winery began in 1874, when it was founded by John Thomann. By 1880 Thomann was producing 200,000 gallons of wine and 20,000 gallons of brandy every year. In those days all wine was shipped in barrels to San Francisco for bottling.

In 1947 the winery was bought by the Trinchero family: Bob (wine maker), Roger and their father, Mario. In 1972 they produced 52,000 gallons of wine and their estimate for 1973 was 65,000 gallons but, in order to ensure continued high quality, ultimate annual production levels will not exceed 25,000 cases. Considering that the winery produced at least 50 wine varieties during the 1950s and 1960s, the Trincheros' new policy of producing a limited selection of premium wines represents a significant change of emphasis.

277 St. Helena Highway, St. Helena; (707) 963-3104; daily 9 - 5; tours by appointment.

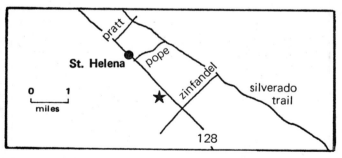

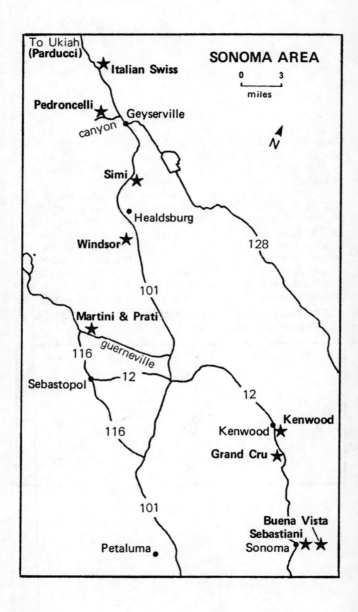

Sonoma /
Mendocino Region

Visitors never cease to marvel at the unspoiled beauty
of the Sonoma Valley, or to question how such an idyllically
pastoral countryside has managed to escape San Francisco's
sprawl. In contrast to the increasing proliferation of residential
developments which until recently plagued the Napa Valley
and many other wine-growing regions on the fringe of the
metropolitan area, Sonoma seems likely to remain one of
the last truly rural pockets of the Bay Area—at least for
a few more years.

Wine production in the Sonoma Valley began in earnest
in the mid-1800s, when Mariano Guadalupe Vallejo (the
famous Mexican general who remained in California after
the American take-over in 1846) and Count Agoston
Haraszthy competed with one another to produce California's
finest wines. Sonoma's dominance of the industry continued
until the 1930s, when it began to lose ground to Napa and
Santa Clara. Today it is the third-largest table wine producing region in California, although increased activity in Mendocino County could someday offer significant competition
to Sonoma.

The region contains an extremely varied selection of
wineries, ranging from small, family-run establishments such
as Grand Cru, Kenwood, Parducci and Pedroncelli to the
larger, better-known wineries of Simi, Buena Vista, Korbel,
Sebastiani and Italian Swiss Colony.

49

Buena Vista

The founder of the Buena Vista winery, Agoston Haraszthy, is known in the wine making world as the father of California viticulture. He was born in 1813 in Fattak, Hungary, and died at the age of 56 in Nicaragua. It's reported that he expired somewhat dramatically by falling from a branch of a tree into the waiting jaws of an alligator—an exciting conclusion to an exceptionally active life: he was secretary to the viceroy of Hungary and an active participant in the Hungarian revolution (where he lost all his vineyards); upon arriving in the States, he founded a town (Sauk City, Wisconsin), served as sheriff of San Diego and first director of the San Francisco Mint and, finally, founded the Buena Vista vineyard, which was built using Chinese labor in 1857.

At one point during his career, Haraszthy was commissioned by the government to bring back vines from Europe to replace the inferior stock then being used by California vintners. He returned with 100,000 rootstocks, which cost him approximately $9,000 plus almost $2,000 for the Wells Fargo delivery. Due to the confusion of the Civil War, he was never repaid, but the vines were distributed to wineries throughout the Sonoma Valley.

Shortly after Haraszthy died in 1869, his winery, Buena Vista, which had become one of the largest in the world, was devastated by the root-louse phylloxera, which swept throughout California and destroyed most of its vineyards. When the 1906 earthquake struck, the Haraszthy family abandoned the winery in despair. In 1943, Frank Bartholomew, chairman of the board of United Press International, bought the winery and land for a mere $17,000. Spending several hundred thousand dollars, he renovated the winery and replanted the destroyed vineyards. In 1968, the winery was bought by Young's Market Company, a Los Angeles-based wholesaler of wine, spirits and gourmet groceries.

Today the ivy-clad stone winery, surrounded by picturesque picnic areas, is an official historical monument. The cellar tasting room, which dates back to 1857, is sometimes a little wet, since the mountain leaks! Here, in addition to selling gifts and sandwiches, Buena Vista offers an extensive selection of wines for tasting, including its prime varietals (when available): Johannisberg Riesling, Cabernet Sauvignon and Gewürztraminer.

18000 Old Winery Road, Sonoma; (707) 938-8504; daily 9:30 - 5; informal tours; pleasant picnic area.

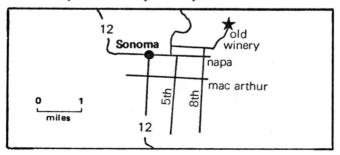

Grand Cru

Grand Cru is a small corporation headed by five people: Allen Ferrera and Bob Magnani handle the wine making, and Russell Taft, Charles Balassi and Joseph Nichelini are at the business end.

This winery dates back to 1886, when it was built by a Frenchman, Francois Lamoine. Using vine cuttings from his native land, he operated the winery from 1890 until about 1910 when a series of unexplainable fires led him to abandon the winery. It remained untouched until 1925 when it was purchased by Felix Mancuso. At that time the winery was designed for the production of bulk generic wines.

In 1970 the present owners arrived. Allen Ferrera gave up his secure 9 to 5 job at an optical firm in Berkeley and became totally involved in rebuilding the winery. Bob Magnani, the wine maker, works at the winery on evenings and weekends. He started wine making as a hobby, learning from an uncle who had studied the art in Italy, and later in California. They released their first two wines in 1972.

Grand Cru vineyards has a modern, homey tasting room with a spiral staircase. The outdoor deck area with its tables and chairs overlooks a magnificent view of the Sonoma Valley and is an extremely pleasant place to spend a summer afternoon. Under the house is a series of concrete wine-aging tanks dating back to Lamoine's days, some of which have a capacity of more than 17,000 gallons. Recent renovations have provided doorway entrances, and they are now used to store and age barreled wines.

Zinfandel Blanc de Noir (a rare wine produced by only two other wineries in California), Zinfandel Rosé (an unusually dark, heavy varietal) and Zinfandel Coulant are Grand Cru's only three wines to date, but soon more will be added. A visit to this small winery should prove interesting and informative, because its employees are willing to take the time to explain their wine making procedures. Be sure to notice the exceptionally informative back labels on their bottled wines.

1 Vintage Lane, Glen Ellen; (707) 966-8100; weekends and holidays 10 - 5; informal tours.

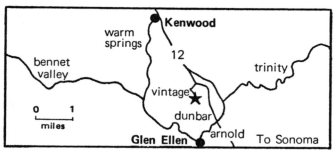

Italian Swiss Colony

Italian Swiss takes the wine-tasting business seriously. Even the delicately landscaped parking lots cannot disguise the fact that the winery expects, and gets, a massive traffic in tourist trade. In 1972 alone, more than 300,000 visitors passed through its three tasting rooms to the accompaniment of soft background music and regular loudspeaker announcements of departing winery tours. The guides here are dressed like Alpine mountaineers.

Italian Swiss began as a colony for unemployed Swiss and Italian workers who poured into California during the middle 1800s. The colony was the idea of Swiss-born Andrea Sbarbaro, who until 1873 ran his own store in San Francisco. In 1875 he helped organize a mutual loan association to provide financial assistance to the jobless immigrants; by 1881 he, along with other businessmen, had amassed $10,000 and used it to buy land in Sonoma County. The place so reminded them of their homeland that they christened it Asti, after a town of that name in Italy. The land was prepared for growing vines, and immigrants were offered room and board in return for their farming services at $35 a month. Five dollars of each employee's salary was retained as an installment contribution towards eventual ownership of his own plot.

Since those early days the winery passed through many hands, until in 1953 it was sold to United Vintners, Inc., a subsidiary of Heublein. Within the broad encompassing arms of this organization are found labels such as Mission Bell, Inglenook, Petri, Lejone, Hartley, Jacques Bonet, Carnival, Chateau Louis, Santa Fe . . . and the list goes on. The company's philosophy is to promote a mass-media appeal through television and magazine advertising. In addition to its pop wines, for which Italian Swiss is particularly noted, the company is especially proud of its private stock offerings: burgundy, chablis, Grenache Rosé.

Asti; (707) 894-2541; daily 8 - 5, summer 8 - 6:30; guided tours.

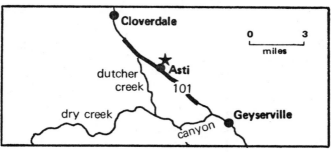

Kenwood

Until a very short time ago Kenwood wines could only be purchased in bulk at the winery. That was during Julius Pagani's days. He was the son of John, and nephew of Armadeo Pagani, two Italian pioneers who built the original winery in 1906. Shortly after Prohibition Julius Pagani devoted his time to rebuilding the winery and soon found himself with a local following. Julius died in 1969 and the winery passed to his brother John, a dean at the University of Santa Clara.

Learning that the winery was for sale, the Lees, a young San Francisco family with little experience in wine making, purchased it in 1970 with brother-in-law John Sheela and close friend Neil Knott. Bob Kozlowski, whom the family had met on a camping trip, is the winemaster, and energetic Mike Lee is the cellarmaster. His father, Martin Lee, was the chief of inspectors for the San Francisco police department until his recent retirement.

During Julius Pagani's days the winery produced 180,000 gallons of wine annually. Today, the yearly total is only 40,000 gallons, but the Lees hope to reach 100,000 and still

maintain the image of a small family-run winery. Although Kenwood wines are now available throughout California, a fair amount is held in reserve for Pagani's original customers, who are still the most loyal supporters of the winery.

1970 was the first production year for the Lees. They are enthusiastic about all the wines they have prepared, a selection of which can be tasted at a corner table in the aging room. Zinfandel, burgundy, Grey Riesling and Chenin Blanc are four of their prime recommendations.

9592 Sonoma Highway, Kenwood; (707) 833-5891; daily 9 - 5; informal tours.

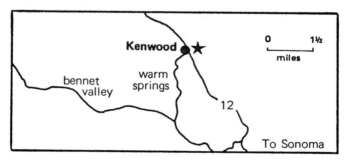

Korbel

In 1862 Francis, Anton and Joseph Korbel, all qualified engineers from Czechoslovakia, founded the Korbel champagne cellars on the banks of the Russian River near Guerneville. In addition to the stately ivy-clad building which faces the main road, the complex includes the original winery built in 1862, an ornate tower (replica of a prison tower which was once the temporary home of one of the brothers in Czechoslovakia and which was used to house the brandy distrillery until 1942) and an old Northwestern Pacific railroad station which dates back to 1876. The brothers purchased the terminal in 1935 for a mere $5.

The winery was sold in 1954 to the Heck brothers, whose father, Adolf Heck, Sr., was vice-president of the American Wine Co. in St. Louis. The brothers have made few changes with the exception of adding an extremely attractive tasting room.

The Korbel winery is known for its excellent champagnes and more recently, brandy and wines. The traditional *champenoise* method of making champagne is still used but with subtle modifications. Previously, the bottles were turned by hand; now they are turned by an automatic vibrating mechanism every six hours. This variation has not only increased production but, in the opinion of the Heck brothers, has also removed the chance of human error, thereby assuring that each bottle of champagne will receive consistent treatment. In addition, the disgorging is no longer done by hand, but by machine. Prior to its acquisition by the Heck brothers, the winery was producing only 5,400 cases a year and boasted seven employees. In 1972 it produced 318,000 cases and now has 75 employees.

The Korbel tours are thorough and instructive. The winery's fascinating history, along with champagne production, is described in full. At the close of the tour visitors are led to the new tasting room and presented with a selection of champagne and dinner wines. Natural and brut champagne, along with Cabernet Sauvignon, a new Zinfandel and Grey Riesling are considered by Hecks to be their finest wines.

River Road, Rio Nido near Guerneville; (707) 887-2294; daily 10 - 4:30; tours at 10:30, 1:00, and 2:30.

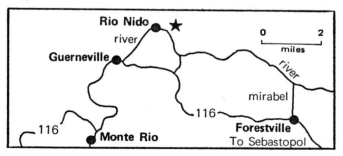

Martini & Prati

Known as the Twin Fir Winery during the 1880s, Martini & Prati was purchased by Rafaelo Martini, an artichoke farmer and immigrant from Italy, in 1902. Between 1943 and 1950, the winery was owned by W. A. Taylor and Co. (distillers and importers). In 1950 the property was returned to Elmo Martini and his partner, Enrico Prati, who had previously been associated with Italian Swiss Colony, and the winery has since remained in the hands of the Martini family.

Martini & Prati concentrates on the production of generic wines, and almost all its stock is sold in bulk to other wineries in the area. The limited amount of wine which remains for its own distribution is bottled under the Martini & Prati and Fountaingrove labels. The latter label was bought during the 1950s from a famous Santa Rosa winery (no longer in existence) then owned by Prince K. Nagasawa. This gentleman was a member of the Brother-

hood of the New Life, a utopian spiritual society that had founded the Fountaingrove winery in the 1880s.

The tasting room here is more like a storage area, but there's a lengthy bar. Although the winery is naturally proud of everything it produces, we found the Zinfandel and sweet vermouth especially worthy of note.

2191 Laguna Road, Santa Rosa; (707) 823-2404; Mon. - Fri. 9 - 4; tours by appointment Sat. & Sun.

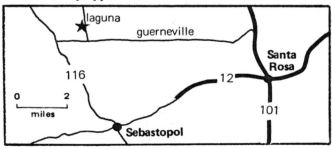

Parducci

Located in a cool canyon in the northern part of the picturesque Ukiah Valley, the Parducci Wine Cellars is owned by two brothers, John and George Parducci. John Parducci has been blessed with the pioneer spirit. To many in the area, he's known as the father of premium varietal grapes in Lake County, a reputation he probably acquired when he instigated the first plantings of Cabernet Sauvignon in 1966.

All Parducci wines are available for tasting. The Pinot Chardonnay, Cabernet Sauvignon, Pinot Noir and their specialty, the French Colombard, are considered by John Parducci and his new winemaster, Joe Monostori, to be among their best. The Parducci brothers believe that wines should be naturally stablized rather than filtered; they are racked many times during the aging period in accordance with the Parduccis' motto that nature is the best wine maker. Appropriately, therefore, Parducci wines tend to be extremely rich and full-bodied.

501 Parducci Road, Ukiah; (707) 462-3828; daily 9 - 5.

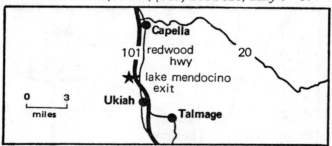

Pedroncelli

This small winery tucked away in the rolling hills west of Geyserville is owned and operated by the Pedroncelli family, whose head, John Pedroncelli, founded it in 1927. From a hobby of wine making he bought a few acres of vines and began selling his produce to the local wineries. In 1934 he went into wine making on a commercial basis. His business grew and in 1963 he passed it on to his two sons, John and Jim. The J. Pedroncelli Winery has continued to flourish and although the old winery built by John, Sr. still remains, many additions and improvements have been made.

The tasting section is tucked into a corner of the huge storage room. There's always a warm welcome—usually by one of the family. It's truly a family enterprise; each member makes his own significant contribution. Most of the wines are available for tasting, and the Pedroncellis are particularly proud of their Zinfandel, Zinfandel Rosé, burgundy, chablis, Chenin Blanc, Pinot Noir and Cabernet Sauvignon. All the varietals are vintage dated.

The Pedroncellis concentrate on the production of classical varietals. The grapes come from either their own or adjacent hillside vineyards. This they consider especially important to the success and high quality of their wines.

1220 Canyon Road, Geyserville; (707) 857-3619; daily 9 - 5; informal tours.

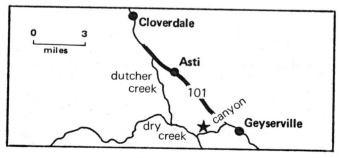

Sebastiani

At the age of 14 a penniless Samuele Sebastiani arrived in Sonoma from Tuscany, Italy. The year was 1893. After helping build the Sonoma City Hall by quarrying stone in the area, he soon turned to what he had always considered just a dream—wine making. In 1904 he bought a hand-operated press, purchased grapes from local Italian farmers, made 500 gallons of Zinfandel and sold the wine back to the same farmers. Within a short time he had built his own winery, provided homes for his workers and even helped finance the paving of Sonoma's streets.

Today the winery is still family-owned. August Sebastiani and his wife Sylvia (author of the recently published cookbook *Mangiamo,* translated: "let's eat") took over the winery when his father died in 1944, and August's son, Sam, later joined the winery as general manager.

The tasting room looks like an Old English pub, but is actually part of the stone cellars built during Samuele's days. The 18-inch thick limestone walls enclose 6,000 barrels: 50-gallon redwood barrels are used for the aging of red

wine, and American white oak for the aging of white wine. A few casks have been intricately carved by 72-year-old Earle Brown, who rambled into the winery during his retirement in 1966.

From the extensive range of wines available for tasting, the Green Hungarian 1967, Barbera (for which the winery is so well known), Gamay Beaujolais, Zinfandel, White Johannisberg Riesling (aged for approximately three years) and Gewürztraminer are some of the family's favorites.

389 Fourth Street East, Sonoma; (707) 938-5532; daily 9 - 5; guided tours.

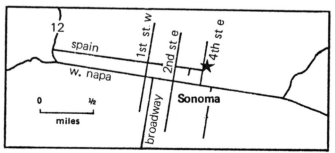

Simi

The Simi Winery is located in a particularly scenic part of the northern Sonoma Valley. It is now owned by Russell Green, who, prior to buying the old winery, was president of Signal Oil. Since he took over in 1970, production has increased dramatically and a well-designed tasting room has been built, partially constructed of wood taken from the winery's old redwood aging tanks that date back to 1876.

Most of Simi's grapes are grown in the nearby Alexander Valley, an area considered by many professionals in the wine industry to produce grapes with outstanding color and tannin characteristics. Russell Green says of the Alexander Valley: "We expect it to become a wine name of renown."

There's an impressive range of dinner wines including Gewürztraminer, Johannisberg Riesling, Zinfandel, Cabernet Sauvignon and Carignan, in addition to an unusual Rosé of Cabernet Sauvignon. Simi is now vintage-dating its white wines, and will follow with vintage-dated reds in 1974. Andre Tchelistcheff, who recently retired after 38 years as winemaster at Beaulieu, now serves Simi as consultant enologist and technical adviser.

Healdsburg Avenue, Healdsburg; (707) 433-4276; daily 9 - 5; guided tours.

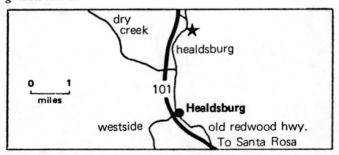

Windsor

In a small Victorian house in Tiburon, reportedly at one time a house of ill repute, Rodney Strong and his wife, Charlotte, founded Tiburon Vintners in 1960. Rodney Strong was once the leading male dancer for the Lido in Paris and during his time in Europe he visited many of the wine growing areas which engendered an enthusiasm for wine making. After returning to the U.S., he purchased the present tasting facilities in Tiburon, and developed an unusual personalized labeling concept: wine can be ordered with a customer's own name on the label. From a clientele of 400, the mailing list has climbed today to more than 280,000. Following the Tiburon winery's rapid success, the Strongs founded, in 1970, the new Windsor winery 50 miles north of the Bay Area.

The winery was designed in the shape of a cross. The circular tasting room on the second floor has observation balconies from which visitors can view the working area below. A Greek theater offers cultural facilities throughout the summer, and cooking classes are held between April

and October by Yvonne Boulleray, who is also the *maitre de cuisine* for privately held gourmet lunch and dinner parties. The winery also houses a full-time printing section where all the wine labels, pamphlets and newsletters are produced, and there's a large, pleasant picnic area.

From Windsor's extensive range of red, white and champagne wines, the Chardonnay, Cabernet Sauvignon, Grenache Rosé and *brut* champagne are considered highlights.

11455 Old Redwood Highway, Healdsburg; (707) 433-5545; daily 10 - 5; tours on request.

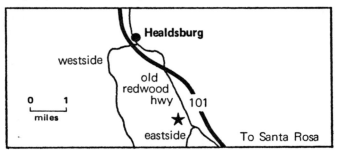

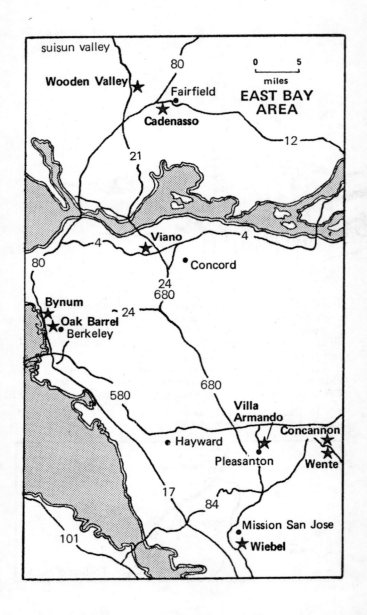

suisun valley

Wooden Valley ★

80

● Fairfield

Cadenasso ★

EAST BAY AREA

0   5
miles

12

21

Viano ★

● Concord

4   4

80

24
680

Bynum ★

Oak Barrel ★
● Berkeley

24

680

580

Villa Armando ★

Concannon ★

● Hayward

★ Pleasanton

Wente ★

17

84

Mission San Jose ●

Wiebel ★

101

Livermore Valley / East Bay Region

The well-drained gravel soils of the Livermore Valley region have long produced some of California's finest white wines, similar in character to those found in the Garonne River district of Bordeaux, France.

The area's development as a wine-growing region began in the 1880s when railroad magnate Leland Stanford planted 350 acres of vines at his Warm Springs resort near Mission San Jose and successful results prompted others to plant vineyards and establish wineries in the area.

Today some of the better-known wineries in the region include Wente, Weibel (famous for its champagne), Concannon and Villa Armando (which retails the bulk of its production on the East Coast).

Further to the north, around Martinez, are a few hardy remnants of the extensive wine production industry that once flourished there. The Conrad Viano, Cadenasso and Wooden Valley wineries are all small family concerns that continue to hold their own against the impact of the metropolitan Bay Area's eastward expansion.

Cadenasso

An incorrigible story-teller with an ear-to-ear smile, wine maker Frank Cadenasso does most of the talking in his tasting room. The Cadenasso Winery near U.C. Davis is the only producing one in Solano County, and the only one in its diocese to have received ecclesiastical permission to make altar wines.

Until recently Frank Cadenasso and his family owned about 200 acres of vineyards, but in order to keep up with demand they have purchased still more land. From a production of 100,000 gallons of varietals a year, Cabernet Sauvignon stands out as Frank's personal choice. Grey Riesling, Zinfandel, Chenin Blanc, Pinot Noir and Grignolino are all available. Much of his wine is prepared for other, better-known wineries.

The Cadenasso Winery was founded in 1906 when Giovanni Cadenasso, Frank's father, arrived from Italy. From its original location on the Rutherford ranch in the Green Valley, the winery was moved to Fairfield and established at its present site in 1926.

The concrete-tunneled entrance and pink-walled tasting room provide an informal setting for the avid groups of wine lovers who flock here on weekends. Changes are imminent, however: Frank Cadenasso intends to expand. A new winery is due to open on U. S. 80 at Abernathy Road in Fairfield sometime in August, 1974. The old tasting room will then be closed, but the Cadenassos intend to continue the tasting, and probably also run tours, in the new building.

On Texas, Fairfield; (707) 425-5845; daily 8 - 6; no tours to date.

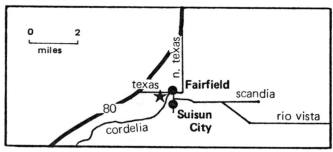

Concannon

This winery, now a registered historical landmark, was founded by an Irishman, James Concannon, in 1883. In 1964 Jim and Joe Concannon, two active members of the family-owned corporation, made their own history in the Livermore area by pioneering Petite Sirah as a red varietal. This area had always been well known for its outstanding white wines, whereas reds had been used for blending only. The idea of producing a premium red varietal was received skeptically by others in the industry, but the brothers won out: Petite Sirah was a tremendous success and is now one of their best sellers. The wine ages for approximately three years, and for five years during an exceptional vintage.

The tasting area is in the middle of the aging and bottling cellars, where the atmosphere is informal and welcoming. The Concannons' recommended wines to date are Zinfandel Rosé, a 100-percent Cabernet Sauvignon that has been bottle-aged for five years, their Prelude Dry Sherry and, of course, their outstanding Petite Sirah.

Tesla Road at Livermore Avenue, Livermore; (415) 477-3760; Mon. - Sat. 9 - 4, Sun. 12 - 4:30; tours at 9, 10, 11, 1, 2, 3, Mon. - Fri.

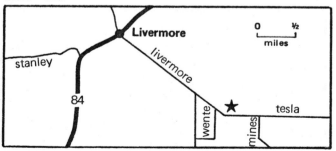

Bynum

Finding the small but active Bynum Winery on busy San Pablo Avenue in Albany is totally unexpected. The sales/tasting room is stocked with home wine and beer-making supplies produced by California Vintners—a separate business founded by former newspaperman Davis Bynum, who is also the founder, wine maker and owner of the Bynum Winery.

Davis's father, Lindley Bynum, is well known for his book *California Wines and How to Enjoy Them*. Because of his father's interest in wines, Davis Bynum was virtually weaned on Cabernet Sauvignon. In 1967 he began producing his own wines, starting by buying wines in bulk and bottling them on the premises. Bynum just purchased an additional 82 acre parcel near Healdsburg in Sonoma County for future production. However all tastings and retail sales will remain at the Albany site.

From his extensive list of wines, for the Barefoot Bynum Burgundy, Zinfandel, Cabernet Sauvignon, Barbera, Colombard, Traminer and Petite Sirah Rosé are considered some of the best to date.

614 San Pablo Avenue, Albany; (415) 526-1366; guided tours when staff available.

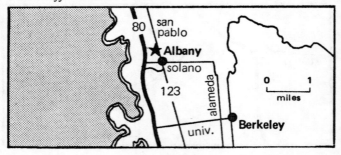

Oak Barrel

Oak Barrel cellars is a very small winery, which is almost unique in that it still operates within city limits. Its own range of wines is neatly displayed along with those from many competitors, including Almaden, Simi, Paul Masson, San Martin, Weibel, Pedroncelli and Cuvaison.

Wines with the Oak Barrel label are available only at the winery, and the list is exceptionally long. Books on wine making, home brewing and cooking, in addition to all the equipment you're likely to need to set up your own home wine and beer production are on display. You can rent a barrel, fill your own bottles from the cellar's wine and sherry casks, or buy endless varieties of herb vinegar—rosemary, basil, French onion, garlic, dill, parsley, etc. Also note the fascinating selection of attractive but functional European oak barrels.

Although not all Oak Barrel wines are available for sampling, visitors can expect a reasonable choice from its selection of premium wines.

1201 University Avenue, Berkeley; (415) 849-0400; 10 - 7 Mon. - Sat., 11 - 7 Sun.; no tours.

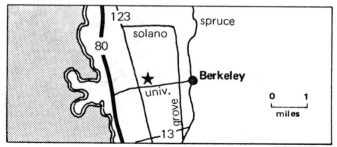

Conrad Viano

Directional signs that read "Grape Hill" recall the past history of an area once rich in vineyards. However, the vineyards of the Conrad Viano Winery, consisting of approximately 60 acres, are the only significant ones now remaining here. Housing developments and high property taxes have helped erase previous wineries from the map. But Viano's stands firm.

Clement Viano, grandson and namesake of the late

founder, is a jovial farmer who today operates the winery with his father, Conrad. Both have experimented with the production of red and white varietals. Although some Viano wines are sold to restaurants in the area, most are distributed from the tiny homey basement tasting room, where Mrs. Carmen Viano is usually in charge.

Zinfandel (of which the family is especially proud), burgundy, chablis, Zinfandel Rosé and Grenache Rosé are all available for sampling. The rosés are particularly unusual in that they are aged for as long as five years, as opposed to the six-month to one-year aging period favored by most vintners.

150 Morello Avenue, Martinez; (415) 228-0288; daily 9 - 5; no tours.

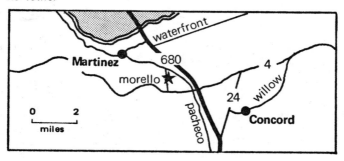

Villa Armando

Villa Armando is a well-established winery hidden in the heart of Pleasanton. To most Californians, its name may be unfamiliar, since almost all Villa Armando wines are shipped to the East Coast. (If you happen to be dining out in Greenwich Village, particularly in one of its many Italian restaurant there's a good chance that you'll be served Villa Armando wines.)

The Villa Armando Winery was founded in 1903 by Frank Garatti, a native of Italy. In 1948 Garatti's son-in-law, F. W. Brenner, took over until Brenner's death in 1960, when the winery was purchased by Anthony D. Scotto, the present owner. Scotto commutes between New York and Pleasanton with occasional side trips to Italy as director of the Valentina Wine Company in Rome.

Many of the wines produced here are somewhat different in character than most California wines, as evidenced by Vino Rustico (based on an old Italian recipe), Orobianco (a white and fruity wine) and Rubinello. Its more familiar Pinot Noir

was mentioned as a recommended wine in the June, 1972 issue of *Vintage Magazine*. Other notable products include a Valentina vermouth (a full line of Valentina wines is expected to appear in the very near future), and a Ruby Cabernet which is due to be released in the fall of 1973.

Notice the Italian ceramics and beautiful cameos on sale in the delightful, Spanish-style tasting room. These are a recent addition, and brought from Italy by Scotto's wife.

553 St. John Street, Pleasanton; (415) 846-5488; 10 - 5 Mon. Sat., noon - 5 Sun.; no tours.

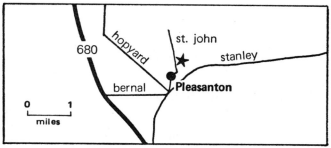

PINOT NOIR

by

Weibel

*For three generations our family has made this
magnificent wine from the aristocratic Pinot noir grape.
Its full, rich body and elegant softness harmonize
superbly with all robust foods.*

Fred Weibel

ALC. 12% BY VOL.

Weibel Champagne Vineyards · Mission San Jose, Calif.

Weibel

The bumpy drive along the pot-holed road leading to the
Weibel winery doesn't last too long. The tasting room, set
in a grove of trees and designed as a hunting lodge, boasts
an historical landmark commemorating Leland Stanford's
residence on the estate during the 1860s. Stanford had
built an elaborate resort hotel and spa for wealthy Californians. After the complex literally fell apart during the 1868
earthquake, Stanford and his brother began a new venture—
grape growing and the production of wine.

The Weibel family entered the picture in 1939 when they opened the Weibel Champagne Vineyards. At the time of writing, the winery is still owned by the Weibels, although rumors abound of multimillion-dollar take-over bids. Their wine list is evenly divided between sparkling, white and red dinner wines, with a smaller selection of sherries and dessert wines also available. Heavy emphasis, however, is placed on the preparation of champagne by the Charmat (bulk) process for restaurants and hotels. (A total of 600 personalized labels are used for this purpose.) The champagne that appears under the Weibel label is reportedly produced by the *champenoise* method (naturally fermented in the bottle), although this production area is not visited during the tour.

Wines the Weibels consider of exceptional merit are their Crackling Rosé, Pinot Chardonnay, Green Hungarian, Johannisberg Riesling, Pinot Noir, Cabernet Sauvignon, Gamay Beaujolais and claret. During the past year Weibel released a new wine, Crackling Blanc de Blancs.

Visitors who are willing to leave the pleasant tasting room can take a brief tour of the winery which, unfortunately, tends to be a bit noisy due to the close proximity of the bottling plant. A new tasting room in Ukiah was opened in the summer of 1973, to which an a adjoining winery will eventually be added.

1250 Stanford Avenue, Mission San Jose; (415) 656-2340; daily 10 - 4:30; guided tours during weekdays.

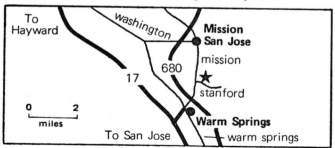

Wente

The Wente Bros. winery is a small corporation consisting of members of the Wente family and a few employees of long-standing. In recent years, modernization in the form of a spacious tasting room and new wine-producing equipment has obliterated most traces of the old winery that was founded by Carl Wente.

CALIFORNIA

Le Blanc de Blancs

A SUPERB BLEND OF
CHENIN BLANC AND UGNI BLANC GRAPES

PRODUCED AND BOTTLED AT THE WINERY BY

WENTE BROS.

ALCOHOL 12½% BY VOLUME   LIVERMORE, CALIFORNIA, U.S.A.

Wente, a native of Hanover, Germany, arrived in California in 1880 and for a short time worked with Charles Krug. In 1883 he started his own winery, producing and selling his wine on a bulk basis to bottlers in San Francisco. In 1915 Wente visited a tasting competition and discovered that—though most of his wines had received awards—because of the contemporary practice whereby bottlers labeled wines under their own names, the Wente name was not mentioned. During Prohibition the winery supplied Georges de Latour, founder of the Beaulieu winery, with sacramental wines, and by 1933 Wente's wine was appearing under 42 different labels. In 1942 the practice of private labeling was discontinued, and the Wente name became truly established.

The Wente vineyards are still located in the Livermore Valley. Because of urban sprawl and increased production demands, the corporation recently purchased an additional 700 acres in the Monterey area. Today Wente makes an average of 250,000 cases a year. The new vineyards will enable the company to increase production substantially.

Although the Livermore area is better known for its outstanding white wines, the Wente Zinfandel (available only at the winery unless you're flying one of the major airlines) is considered by many to be outstanding. Wente's Petite Sirah (introduced recently), Grey Riesling (which accounts for 50 percent of its total West Coast sales) and chablis, (an East Coast favorite) are also considered to be fine, along with its rather unusual Blanc de Blancs.

5565 Tesla Road, Livermore; (415) 447-3603; 9 - 5 Mon. - Sat., 11 - 4 Sun.; tours during the week.

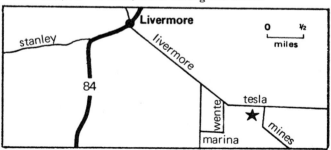

Wooden Valley

Although a small family concern, the Wooden Valley Winery is a busy, popular place, especially with the local residents. Its wines, bottled under the Wooden Valley label, are available only at the simply designed tasting room. Although the winery offers quite a range of varietals (Pinot Noir, Zinfandel, etc.), these have been processed and bottled by other wineries. However, its generics—all of which it is justly proud—are blended and bottled by the family and include Rhine wine (one of the most popular), Golden Chateau, Petite Rosé, Vino Bianco and vin rosé. These are all sold in fifths, half-gallon and gallon bottles.

Mario Lanza (no relation to the late singer) and his son, Richard, are the owners. Members of the Lanza family were

employees of the winery during the 1940s. In 1955 they purchased the place for themselves, and since then have experimented with new wines, one of their first being Barbera.

Suisun Valley Road, Suisun City; (707) 425-3962; daily except Monday 9 - 5:30; no tours.

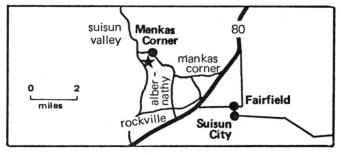

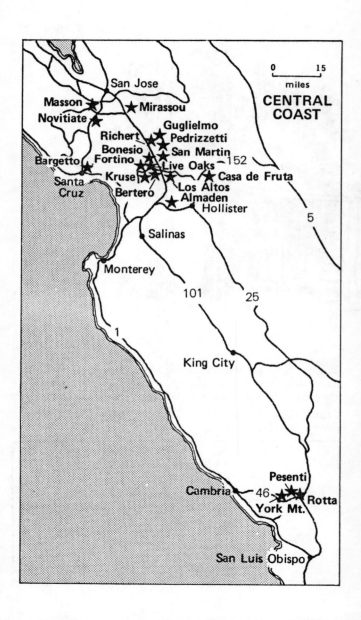

CENTRAL
COAST

0   15
miles

San Jose

Masson
Novitiate

Mirassou

Guglielmo
Pedrizzetti

Richert
Bonesio
Fortino

San Martin

Bargetto

Live Oaks — 152

Santa
Cruz

Kruse
Bertero

Casa de Fruta

Los Altos
Almaden

Hollister

Salinas

5

Monterey

101   25

1

King City

Pesenti

Cambria — 46

Rotta

York Mt.

San Luis Obispo

Santa Clara/ Central Coast Region

This varied region of bayshore, mountains and coastline contains an interesting cross section of winery types. In the mammoth category, this region is the home of the famous Masson and Almaden wineries, both of which have vastly increased their production during the last decade. The small independent establishments are represented by the tiny Richert, Guglielmo and Live Oaks wineries, all located around Gilroy and Highway 101. Others, such as the San Martin winery (visitors are given the fastest seven-wine tasting session on record) and the Casa de Fruta, cater primarily to a large tourist trade. Finally, there are secluded wineries such as the Novitiate of Los Gatos, hidden high in the Santa Cruz Mountains, where wine tasting is combined with a magnificent view of the San Francisco Bay region.

Santa Clara County is the heart of California's Mission Country, and a weekend spent in the area would not be complete without a visit to San Juan Bautista, Mission San Jose or the historic city of Monterey. Gradually, as pressures for urban development increase, a few of the region's wineries may be lost or relocated. However, in contrast to the plight of the Cucamonga region near Los Angeles, such problems here do not appear to be particularly significant yet.

Almaden

In 1852, a Frenchman, Charles Lefranc, planted some vines received from Europe and founded what is now the Almaden Vineyards. The vineyards eventually grew to be the largest in the region. Lefranc married Adel Thee, daughter of Etienne Thee (builder of the Almaden ranch house), and Paul Masson, who had joined Lefranc in the business, married Lefranc's daughter, Louise. Paul Masson broke away to start his own winery and the business passed to Charles Lefranc's son, Henry. Today, Almaden Vineyards is a subsidiary of National Distillers and Chemical Corporation.

Almaden has two tasting rooms. The first, just off the plaza in San Juan Bautista, has been sensitively designed and blends well with its historic surroundings. A gazebo completes the attractive picture. Equally pleasing, the second tasting room is nestled among gently rolling hills on the Pacheco Pass Highway and was designed in the California Mission style. The San Juan Bautista tasting room specializes in gifts and has its own simple shopping arcade.

Almaden produces 43 wines. Mountain Nectar Vin Rosé and Grenache Rosé appear to be its most popular labels. Among the reds, the winery is exceptionally proud of its Pinot Noir, burgundy and Gamay Beaujolais, and of the whites, Gewürztraminer, Pinot Chardonnay and Johannisberg Riesling.

11 Franklin, San Juan Bautista; (408) 623-4848; 8090 Pacheco Pass, 6 miles north of Hollister (junction of State Hwys. 152 & 156); (408) 637-7554; daily 10 - 5; no tours.

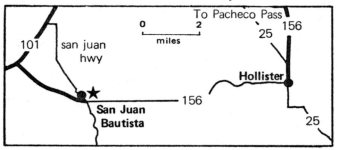

Bargetto

The Bargetto Winery's two-year-old tasting room, brimming with old wine making equipment and ancient family photographs, is located behind the main winery which was founded in 1934 by Phillip Bargetto and his brother John. Today, Lawrence Bargetto, the father of five children, is the president and winemaster. At one time Lawrence seriously considered becoming a physician, but instead found himself studying enology and becoming an associate with his father in the wine business.

All members of the family play a significant role in operating the winery and testing the wines. Patti Ballard, one of the attentive counselors in the tasting room, spends a couple hours every Monday morning giving informal talks on nutrition, cooking and thrifty shopping to local groups and interested visitors. A genuinely enthusiastic wine lover, she takes time and patience to discuss individual wines. There are informal tours and Patti answers any questions regarding the winery, or calls on the experience of

Lawrence Bargetto, the winemaster.

Tasting samples include a tempting selection of fruit wines (all are 100 percent pure fruit). Red and white table wines are also produced, and Moscato Amabile, Dry Muscat, chianti (1963), burgundy (1964), Barbera (1969) and Ruby Cabernet stand out as the family's personal favorites. An additional tasting room is located on Cannery Row in Monterey.

3535 N. Main Street, Soquel; (408) 475-2258; daily 9:30 - 5:30; informal tours.

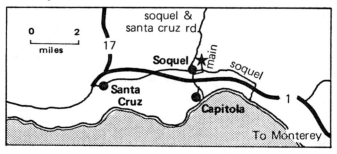

Bertero

Driving past the water tower along the unpaved roadway leading towards the winery, we passed the new rustic Bertero tasting room, which opened in March, 1973. The Bertero Winery itself dates back to 1917, when Alfonso Bertero prepared bulk wine for local wineries and sold grapes to home wine makers. Four years ago the Berteros began bottling under their own label, although a large amount still continues to be sold in bulk.

Since 1917 the winery has remained very much a family concern. Angelo Bertero and his sons, Angelo, Jr. and Carl, are the present owners. They produce an extensive array of red and white table wines: chablis, sauterne, Chenin Blanc, Sauvignon Blanc, Grenache Rosé, burgundy, Zinfandel, Pinot Noir and Cabernet Sauvignon. The two wines for which they are particularly well known are Barbera and Grignolino.

The new tasting room includes a small display of glassware and gifts. In addition to the regular tasting facilities, the winery provides private wine-tasting sessions for groups (advance notice is requested).

3920 Hecker Pass Highway, Gilroy; (408) 842-3032; daily 8 - 6; tours available.

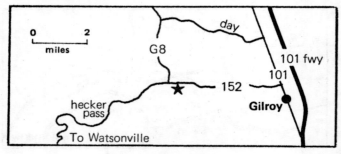

Bonesio

The Bonesio family has been in the California wine making business since 1915. Pietro Bonesio, founder of the present Bonesio Winery, handed it on to his two sons, Louis and Victor, in 1932. Since Victor Bonesio left the winery years ago, Louis and his wife and son, Louis, Jr., have continued the operation. This year (1973), after many years of hard work, they are ready to retire. For this reason, the winery will shortly change hands.

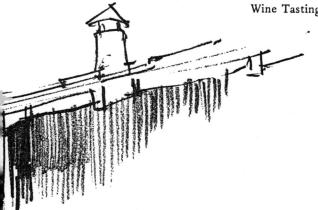

The tasting room at the rear of the more than 100-year-old family home, with an attractive picnic area at the front, was used as a bottling plant until increasing numbers of visitors led to a change about ten years ago. The redwood-tank doorway leads into a cozy, charming room, where all the Bonesio wines bottled with the Uvas (Spanish for grapes) label can be tasted. The vintage wines, Cabernet Sauvignon and Pinot Noir, are considered exceptionally good, and Malvasia Bianca is the family's most unusual wine. Of special note are the Uvas fruit wine selections and a wine vinegar, produced under the Luigi's Pride label. Another tasting room offering Bonesio wines can be found in South Lake Tahoe, California.

1150 Watsonville Road, Gilroy; (408) 842-2601; daily 8 - 6; tours by appointment.

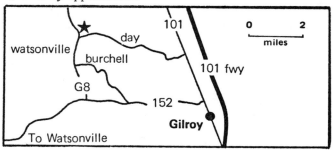

Casa de Fruta

If you're driving along Route 152, Casa de Fruta is a fun place to pause. It is a tourist attraction that offers something for everyone: spacious picnic areas and parking facilities, restaurants, wine, cheese and fruit tasting, gift shops, playgrounds and even wild buffalo. Casa de Fruta dates back to 1908, when the Zanger family planted orchards and opened a roadside fruit stand, but today's recreational complex is a far cry from those humble origins.

6680 Pacheco Pass (Highway 152), Hollister; (408) 637-4781; daily 8:30 - 7:30, during summer 8:30 - 9:00; no tours.

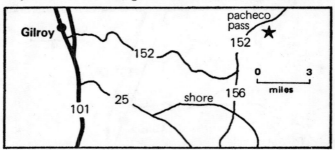

Fortino

Ernest Fortino, third generation of an Italian wine making family, arrived in California twelve years ago and worked with many established wineries in the Santa Clara region before amassing sufficient capital to buy the Cassa Brothers Winery in 1970. After changing the name, Ernest abandoned the old bulk-processing traditions of the winery and, assisted by his wife Maria and their two children, set out to prepare a limited range of select varietal and generic wines. Understandably, their production at the moment is restricted and they're struggling hard to meet customer demands. For this reason, their wines are sold only at the winery.

The tasting room is a tiny, concealed corner of the large working area where Fortino prepares and ages his wines. Tasting is informal and usually hosted by Ernest, who proudly offers his personal favorites, Zinfandel and Grenache Ruby to appreciative visitors. His Cabernet Sauvignon and Petite Sirah also receive much local praise. In addition to the Fortino wines, a small selection of outstanding imported Italian wines is available in the salesroom.

4525 Hecker Pass Highway, Gilroy; (408) 842-3305; daily 9 - 6; informal tours.

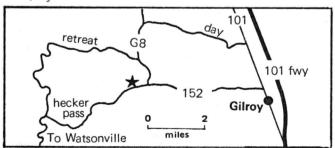

Guglielmo

The third generation of the Guglielmo family is this year launching into vintaged varietals for the first time in its history. The new wines, scheduled for release near the end of 1973 under the Mount Madonna label, include Grignolino Red, Semillon White, Pinot Noir, Ruby Cabernet and Petite Sirah—premium wines the family formerly used only for blending. The Guglielmos will also continue to bottle their private stock of burgundy and sauterne, adding chablis and vin rosé to that line.

Emilio Guglielmo bought his first 25 acres of vineyard in Morgan Hill in 1925, while working at the present winery. He regularly transported his precious harvest of grapes to San Francisco, where he had many friends of French extraction. It was they who eventually advised him to sell wines on a commercial basis under his own label. Thus, in 1933, Emilio Guglielmo became the proud owner of his own small but successful winery. When he died, his son, George, became sole owner and the winery is now operated with the help of George's two sons, George and Gene.

1480 East Main Avenue, Morgan Hill; (408) 779-3064; daily 8 - 5; tours by appointment.

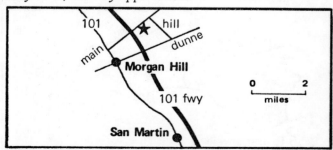

Kruse

Ten years ago Tom Kruse's passion for collecting antiques resulted in his buying a small and very old wine press. In testing his purchase, the inevitable happened and his interest in wines snowballed. Today Tom and his wife, Susan, are the proud owners of a small but promising winery in the shadow of Mount Madonna, near Gilroy.

In September, 1971, having moved into their present home in front of the rambling winery, they produced eight wines for commercial distribution. Zinfandel and Grignolino Rosé are out as their personal favorites, but their bottle-fermented champagne could well rate first place. It's almost unheard of for such newcomers to produce champagne. Tom Kruse, however, is totally enraptured with the entire process, and by the end of 1973 his first champagne production will be available the public. Kruse wines, particularly the reds, tend to be bold in flavor and contain a limited amount of sediment, due to Kruse's abhorrence of excessive filtration and polishing of wines.

Between babying their 33 acres of vineyards, preparing wines and renovating the winery and tasting room, Tom Kruse finds time to teach wine making and wine appreciation classes in the Bay Area. If you're interested in reviving old traditions, inquire about the barefoot grape-crushing contest held at the winery each September and October.

4390 Hecker Pass, Gilroy; (408) 842-7016; daily noon - 6; informal tours; informal picnic area.

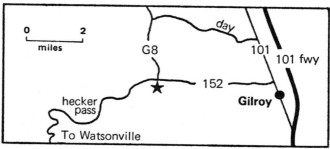

Live Oaks

From the outside, the tasting room of the Live Oaks Winery appears to take up the entire length of the over-sized barn. But inside, it turns out to be a long narrow space divided from the storage and bottling areas. The room is cheerful and full of stuffed birds, animal heads and photographs. The owner, Peter Scagliotti, has a great respect for wildlife and his interest in this subject is almost as intense as his love for wine making. Scagliotti produces premium burgund sauterne and Grenache in addition to his extremely popular wine vinegar, which draws customers from as far afield as Orego

In 1912, Peter's father, Eduardo Scagliotti, founded Live Oaks (named after the numerous oak trees which existed in the area before they were razed to make room for planting vines). He had arrived from Italy in 1900 and worked with Miller and Lux, the famous cattle kings of California. In 1912, he and his brothers, had saved enough money to purchase the E. H. Farmer Ranch—now the Live Oaks Winery. During those early days their most serious problem was ridding the land of the ground squirrels which threatened

to destroy all their plantings. The winery produced wines on a commercial basis until 1917 and the arrival of Prohibition. During that dry era, as did many other wineries, they produced wine for sacramental purposes until they returned to commercial production in 1933. When Eduardo Scagliotti died in 1937, Peter took over.

The Live Oaks premium quality burgundy is considered by many to be especially outstanding, and was rated highly at the San Francisco Wine Sampling Club's 1970 tasting.

3875 Hecker Pass (Highway 152), Gilroy; (408) 842-2401; daily 8 - 5:30; no tours.

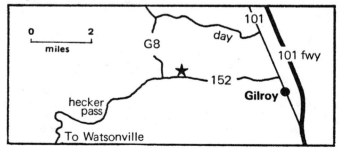

Los Altos

The Los Altos Winery (otherwise known as the B & B Vineyards, Inc.) is owned by the Rapazzini family. In 1960 brothers Jon and Victor Rapazzini, along with their father, Angelo, purchased the old Perelli winery. Today they have three tasting rooms. The Stagecoach Cellars tasting room is only a few months old and has an Old West atmosphere, lots of antiques and an 1875 bar taken from the former Spreckels saloon in downtown San Francisco. The original winery and tasting room, built in 1963, is three miles south of Gilroy on U. S. 101. (The third tasting room is a little inaccessible unless you live in Chicago—it's in Long Grove, Illinois.)

At the moment most Los Altos wines are only available from its tasting rooms, but within the next six months the winery intends to retail throughout the country under its new label, Rapazzini.

Although they buy some bulk wines from other wineries for blending, the Rapazzinis also produce their own and currently offer a wide selection of cocktail, table and dessert wines. Their 18-year-old Family Reserve pale dry sherry, cream sherry and tawny port, although they will be available only for another year or two, are California gold medal winners and considered outstanding, as are their Johannisberg Riesling and Pinot Noir. More popular, however, are their flavored selections: May wine, Ambrosia and Exotica. Personalized wine labels are offered free of charge with a full case of wine. The family also offers an impressive range of Italian, French and German wines in its tasting rooms.

"Stagecoach Cellars," Hwy 101, Aromas; (408) 422-3732; 4350 Monterey Highway, Gilroy; (408) 842-5649; both tasting rooms daily 9 - 6, June - Sept. 9 - 8; no tours.

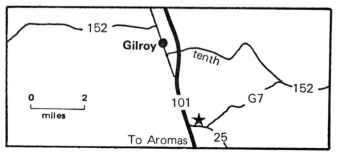

Paul Masson

The Paul Masson Champagne Cellars, built in 1959 and designed by architect John Bolls, is the most modern winery in the region. There are two landmarks: the slim fountain which symbolizes the effervescence of champagne, and the American flag depicting an unmistakable "E"—the President's award for excellence in export sales.

Visitors register for a tour at the reception area. (While walking up the spiral ramp, notice the wine history recorded in mosaic tiles on the face of the ramp—the work of Don Jose Moya del Pino.) Guests are welcomed by a uniformed host who begins the tour with a film show.

Visitors are then led through the plant along observation walkways that overlook the oak, redwood and stainless-steel cooperage,

the bottling plant and stacks of bottle-fermenting champagne. The champagne section is particularly interesting and a full explanation is given of the Masson transfer process—a speedy method of removing sediment from mature champagne prior to final bottling.

The tasting room now awaits the information-saturated guest. The name *Champagne Cellars* may prove misleading, as the winery actually offers a full range of table wines in addition to appetizer, dessert and rare wines. (A recently introduced wine in the latter category is a dry flor sherry.) Emerald Dry, Rhine Castle, Crackling Rosé, Baroque and Rubion are all Masson originals, sold only under the Masson label. Two of these wines, Emerald Dry and Rhine Castle, were developed as a result of research by enologists at the Davis campus of the University of California.

13150 Saratoga Avenue, Saratoga; (408) 257-7800; daily 10 - 4; guided tour.

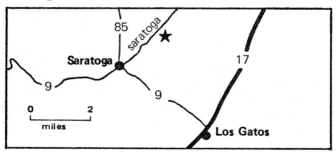

Mirassou

In 1848 Louis Pellier left his home in France and came to California, intent on discovering gold. Instead, he found himself planting vines on the slopes of Mount Hamilton near San Jose. The vines were a success. His brother, Pierre, joined him and brought fine vine cuttings from the Bordeaux area. Pierre Pellier had one child, Henrietta. Pierre Mirassou, a neighboring vintner, married Henrietta in 1881, and shortly afterward the winery was passed on to him.

From 1854 until 1966 the Mirassou wines were sold in bulk to other wineries. During that latter year, the fifth generation of Mirassous decided to launch forth and bottle and market wines under the family name. Developing more vineyards in Soledad, Monterey County (one of the most promising premium grape-growing areas of the future), the Mirassou family expanded the line to include fine premium wines.

In 1970, using a machine developed in conjunction with U. C. Davis which picks, destems and crushes grapes in a matter of seconds, Mirassou produced a Chenin Blanc that won considerable acclaim in the wine world. The winery's

Monterey Riesling, made from the Sylvaner Riesling grape harvested on the Mission Ranch, was introduced in 1972. In the same year, a 1969 Pinot Noir (a dedication bottling honoring Mackie Heuber, wine maker at Mirassou since 1941) was also introduced, along with a 1969 Sparkling Gamay Beaujolais. In 1971 Mirassou released its first Harvest selection (limited bottling) wines: Cabernet Sauvignon, Pinot Noir, Zinfandel, Pinot Chardonnay and Gewürztraminer. These will continue to be released each September along with the winery's more familar offerings.

Aborn Road, San Jose; (408) 374-2000; Mon. - Sat. 10 - 5; Sun. noon - 4; guided tour.

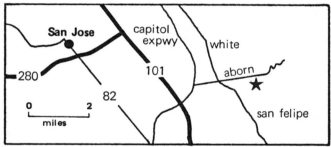

Novitiate
of Los Gatos

There are two Jesuit wineries in the world: Seven Hills, in Australia, and Novitiate Wines in Los Gatos. In 1848, Jesuit missionaries were sent from Turin, Italy, to California and Oregon. Through their work, a college and winery were established in Santa Clara. However, desiring a more serene location for their spiritual needs, the Fathers moved to their present idyllic spot. It was then surrounded by orange groves and a few acres of vineyards—a beautiful setting high in the Santa Cruz mountains with a magnificent panorama of the valley below. The year was 1888. The winery, part of which was built in 1894, still remains today, although subsequent extensions have been added.

During those early days, the Jesuits had two problems: supporting the novices' training, and providing themselves with true altar wines—those that had no added chemicals and were 100 percent grape juice. The winery was founded to meet these needs. Today, approximately 70 percent of its wine is distributed throughout the U. S. for sacramental use, the remainder being sold in California on a commercial basis. All proceeds go to help educate and train the novices for their varied apostolates in the community. Since all wines are made from grapes grown in their own vineyards, the brothers are able to uphold strict quality control over all stages of production.

The tasting, in a dimly lit old stone room, offers a full range of dinner, dessert and aperitif wines. The Novitiate's Black Muscat, made from the Muscat Hamburg grape, a 1964 vintage port and Dry Malvasia, made from a Greek Muscat grape, are considered exceptional wines. Chenin Blanc, Chateau Novitiate (a sweet sauterne), Pinot Blanc, Cabernet Sauvignon and Grenache Rosé are just a few dinner wines of which the Novitiate is particualrly proud.

College and Prospect Avenues, Los Gatos; (408) 354-6471; daily except Sun, and legal holidays 9 - 4; tours at 2 and 3 Tues. and Fri.

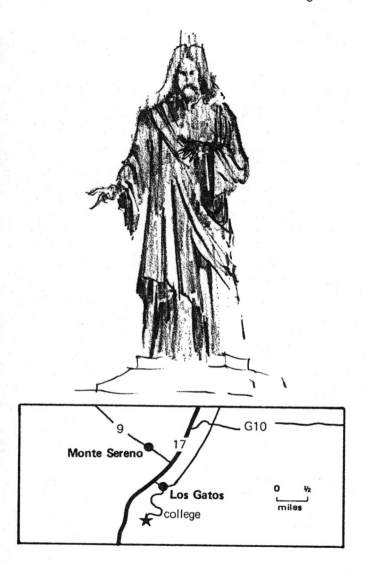

Pedrizzetti

On busy Highway 101, the delightful cellar complex is a perfect spot to take a rest. In quiet courtyard with its picnic tables, you can enjoy a snack of sandwiches from the nearby cellar restaurant and sample the Pedrizzetti wines.

John Pedrizzetti purchased the present winery (about three miles from the tasting room)—in 1945. His son, Edward, took over the winery in 1963. Today, Edward recalls the fun he had making wine in the old days. These last two years have apparently seen a tightening in regulations and an increase in paper work, which have led to difficulties for the small family winery. Edward is therefore selling the winery, although he intends to remain on as winemaster.

Pedrizzetti Winery offers estate-bottled wines, and its Barbera, Green Hungarian and Zinfandel Rosé are considered its best wines to date. The wide selection of dessert and sparkling wines is prepared by another winery.

1645 San Pedro Avenue, Morgan Hill; (408) 779-4512; daily 10 - 6, July - September 9 - 7:30; tours at the winery by appointment.

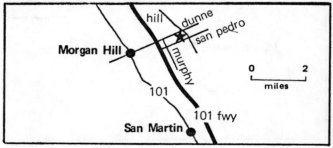

Pesenti

Since 1934, when it was built by founder Frank Pesenti, the winery has been left almost unchanged. The winery is now operated by the third generation of the Pesenti family. Since the first planting of grape vines in 1923, the Pesentis have concentrated on the production of Zinfandel, burgundy, claret and Vino Rosso (a mellow red table wine). Five years ago they released a Cabernet. Today the family ownes 75 acres of vineyards consisting of Zinfandel, muscat, Carignane and Cabernet.

Amidst Pesenti Winery's extensive range of red and white dinner wines are found a few unusual labels: Chateau d'Oro, Chateau Blanc and Vin Rouge. It also offers a tempting range of fruit wines—apple, plum, apricot, cherry, cider, blackberry, loganberry and raspberry—as well as mead, May wine, Tiki Tai and Mokka Lau. The two wines of which the family is especially proud, however, are its Zinfandel and Cabernet. Wines are marketed under the FP (Frank Pesenti) and Pesenti labels. The winery is set in a peaceful country area—a truly delightful place to pause for awhile.

Vineyard Drive, Templeton; (805) 434-1030; daily 8 - 6; tours by appointment.

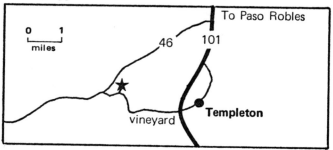

Richert

With tongue-in-cheek humor, evidenced in his "Richert Report" newsletter and advertising pamphlets, Walter Richert—a seemingly modest man—describes himself as "the best sherry blender in California." A graduate of the University of California, he began his work in the wine business in 1935 and was at one time editor of *Wine Review* and *Wines and Vines,* the two trade journals of the industry.

Walter Richert purchases individual wines and blends them at his winery, which is located a few miles from the highway tasting room. That his philosophy—"think as sherry thinks"—has led to success is demonstrated by the numerous awards he has received. Richert's tasting room, in the front section of his home, is ultra-informal, and visitors are at once made comfortably at ease by the host's dry wit.

Although Richert concentrates on the production of ports and sherries, a few years ago he began producing fruit wines of which has apricot wine is especially popular. He is best known for his triple cream sherry, but three other sherries and two ports released by Richert & Sons have been equally praised. All his wines bear the four-barrel trademark symbolizing Walter and his three sons.

18980 Monterey Road, Morgan Hill; (408) 779-3919; daily 10 - 6; no tours.

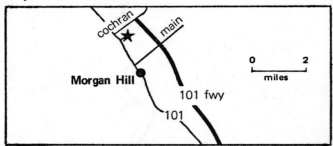

Rotta

The Rotta tasting room, a small, dimly lit place, is cradled in a 7,000-gallon wine tank. This winery was very successful in 1856, when wine was sold to passing travelers and early settlers by its French founder, Adolph Siot. In 1905 the Rotta family, recently arrived from Switzerland, bought the winery. Since the death of her husband, Clement, seven years ago, the place has been managed by Mrs. Romilda Rotta and her son Mervin.

Almost all the Rottas' wines are sold from the tasting room. Their Old Zinfandel, reportedly aged between 14 and 16 years, is appropriately represented by a gold label. Zinfandel would appear to be their prime wine, but sweet and dry muscat, along with two or three vin rosés, are also available.

Vineyard Drive, Templeton; (805) 434-1389; daily 8 - 5, summer 8 - 7; guided tours if staff available.

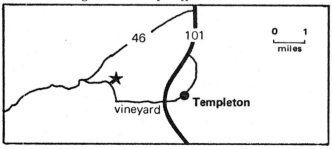

San Martin

A tasting of approximately seven wines, along with a brief introduction to each one, plus a dash round the gift shop— tasting room, will probably take as long as reading this section on the San Martin Vineyards. If you like to taste in a relaxed, easy atmosphere, this is not your kind of place. Due to the bus tours which continually pull into the winery off the U. S. 101, an in-out philosophy seems to be the norm. It's a fast-moving place.

There are San Martin tasting rooms in Monterey, Gilroy (at the Bloomfield Winery), San Jose and San Martin. Its wines are now distributed in 27 states, and although some are sold in bulk, most are bottled under the San Martin label.

The wines San Martin considers to be of special interest are its 1968 Cabernet Sauvignon, 1968 Pinot Noir, Grenache

Rosé, Aprivette (an apricot wine), Gran Pomo (a pomegran-
ate wine) and Mokka Lau (a coffee-flavored wine). Try some
of the delicious wine-cured salami sold in the deli section
of the tasting room in San Martin.

*Highway 101, San Martin; (408) 683-2672; daily 9 - 6;
no tours.*

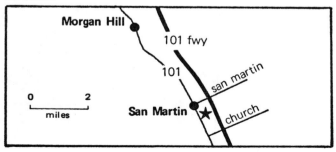

York Mountain

This has to be one of the most attractive of the old wineries in California. The tasting room, once brimming with oak barrels, is today a spacious stone-walled area with a large baronial fireplace. The surrounding valley and the wooded Santa Lucia Mountains provide a truly idyllic setting for this small establishment.

York Mountain Winery has been in operation since 1882, when it was founded by Andrew York. Max Goldman, a past president of the American Society of Enologists, who has been intimately involved with wines for more than 30 years, purchased the winery in 1970. Using his experience and knowledge of the industry, Goldman is expanding and replanting vineyards in order to ensure the ultimate production of the highest-quality premium wines.

Since Max Goldman arrived, he has introduced Cabernet Sauvignon, claret, French Colombard and Chenin Blanc in addition to the winery's long-standing favorites, Zinfandel and burgundy. The dry sherry and five-year old brandy are two highly valued offerings, and 1976 promises to provide

still another: by then, Max expects to have released his one and only York Mountain Extra Dry Champagne.

A particularly pleasant feature of the York Mountain tasting room is that cheese and French bread are usually served as palate-cleansers during the wine sampling. We wish that more wineries would enhance their visitors' enjoyment in this way.

York Mountain Road (off Highway 46,) Templeton; (805) 238-3925; daily 9 - 5; tours by appointment.

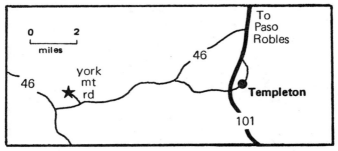

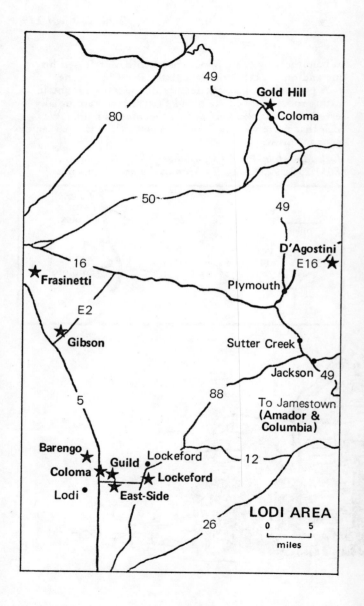

Gold Hill
Coloma

49

80

50

49

D'Agostini
E16

Frasinetti

16

Plymouth

E2

Gibson

Sutter Creek

5

Jackson 49

88

To Jamestown
(Amador &
Columbia)

Barengo
Coloma

Guild

Lockeford

Lockeford

12

Lodi

East-Side

LODI AREA

26

0   5

miles

Lodi Region

The area is divided naturally into two distinct subregions: the flat valley lands around Lodi and Sacramento and the rolling Sierra foothills of the Gold Rush Country. Autumn is a particularly memorable time to visit the valley around Lodi when the vineyards are ablaze with the brilliance of the Flame Tokay vines as they finally reach maturity. Although action at the wineries is somewhat subdued, the best time to visit the foothills is during early spring, when the scorched brown grasses of summer have regained their fresh greenness and Route 49, normally clogged with tourists, is relatively free of traffic.

Until the mid-1960s the Lodi area was primarily a center for the production of dessert wines such as sherry, port and tokay (a blend of sherry and port). However, as the relative demand for these sweet wines decreased, new grape varieties developed by the University of California at Davis and other table-wine grapes were planted. The result has been a significant recent output of table wines by such area establishments as Lockeford, East-Side, Frasinetti and Guild. The variety of microclimates in the Sierra foothills has permitted the production of an interesting array of generic and varietal wines by the region's small wineries, notably d'Agostini, Gold Hill and Columbia.

Amador

The quaint stone structure behind the main street in Amador shelters the cellar-style tasting room and a small wine making area. The tour of the winery—where the procedures are just one step removed from home brewing—can be completed in a matter of minutes by peering around corners into the back section of the building. It's here that Lee Merrill and Harry Ahrendt, the owners of the winery, prepare, bottle and label the wines—truly a two man show!

Numerous personalized labels are their pride and specialty, but look for the Golden Nugget label which is the winery's brand name. If you are in the area, stop in and try a glass of Zinfandel, Sutter's Gold or one of their other unusual wines.

Route 49, Amador City; (209) 267-5320; daily except Wed. 11 - 5; brief tours.

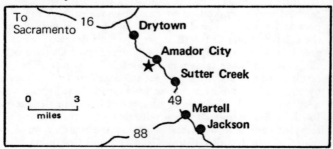

Barengo

Dino Barengo, the jovial owner of Barengo Cellars has been involved with the winery since the early 1940s, when it was a stock corporation and Cesare Mondavi (see Charles Krug) was president. Barengo purchased the winery in 1944. For many years, he was the wine maker, general manager and wine pioneer, being the first vintner in California to produce and bottle Ruby Cabernet in the 1950s. Although the winery has recently been sold to a group of businessmen, Dino Barengo plans to continue in a consulting capacity for the next five years.

The tasting room is charming. Especially inviting on a cold winter day is the roaring fire in the old fireplace. A few tasting highlights recommended by Dino, in addition to the Ruby Cabernet, are the 1964 Pale Dry Sherry, Ruby Port (which is now being bottled from 1959 stock) and May wine, a white table generic (well known in Germany) flavored with woodruff. Barengo's Pedro Ximinez, a triple cream sherry, is unusual in that Dino apparently bought the last planting of Pedro Ximinez grapes in Southern California; after the next bottling, this 15 year-old sherry will reportedly no longer be available. An interesting side feature at Barengo's is the Lodi Art Show, which is held in the cellars on the weekend prior to Memorial Day.

Acampo Road, Acampo; (209) 369-2746; daily 10 - 5; guided tours.

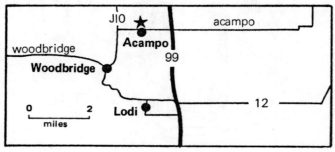

Coloma

The Alexander family once had a thriving winery. Today it has no winery, but a number of tasting rooms including the Coloma Wine Cellars, which the Alexanders purchased in 1965. In July, 1972, the Alexander Winery and tasting room in Lodi, founded in 1935 by Christ Alexander, were razed to the ground by fire, destroying many years of work, all the company's equipment and approximately $120,000 in wine. It was a tragic loss.

One of the visitors's first impressions upon entering Coloma Cellars is the delightful aroma of cheese, which emanates from a large food display. Wine tasting is offered from a range of Coloma dinner wines (including Pinot Chardonnay, Johannisberg Riesling, Green Hungarian, Riesling and Gamay Beaujolais), dessert wines and Alexander dinner wines. Unfortunately, because of the recent fire, all these wines have been purchased from other wineries. No Alexander wine remains—not even the Greek wines, Retsina and Kikineli for which the family is so well known.

In 1969 the Alexanders branched out into making fruit concentrates, which are sold to Wine-Art, America's leading source of home wine making supplies. Coloma Cellars carries a full range of Wine-Art supplies, along with candles, spices, posters and many tempting cheeses.

Highway 99 Frontage Road, 1 mile north of Lodi; (209) 368-2996; daily 9 - 5; no tours.

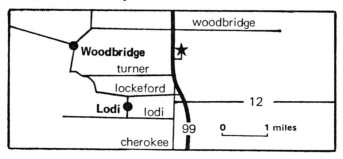

Columbia

Columbia Cellars, way up in the Gold Country, was founded in the tiny Gold Rush town of Columbia in 1970. A short while ago it was moved to Jamestown, which is a far better location from a business viewpoint. The owners, Spencer Hoffman and his wife, are responsible for every facet of operations, from making the wines to bottling and labeling them, dressing the tasting room and acting as hosts to their many visitors. Spencer Hoffman enthusiastically recommends a visit to his winery—if not to buy his wines, at least to admire his huge burned-wood bar.

Prior to starting his own winery, Hoffman worked for a while with Italian Swiss Colony. He produces a standard line of red and white dinner wines, but he also concentrates on the unusual. His Columbian Gold is a sweet wine with a slight raspberry flavor. The Spice Jubilee has a burgundy base to which ten herbs and spices have been added.

Highway 49 at Highway 108, Jamestown; (209) 984-3737; daily, except Tues. 10 - 6; informal tours.

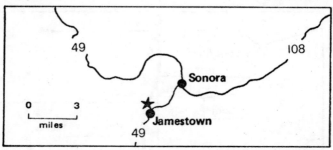

D'Agostini

Gnarled vineyards encircle the d'Agostini Winery. It dates
back to 1856, when Swiss-born Adam Uhlinger erected
the buildings, planted vines and made the first wine. The
d'Agostini family acquired the winery and the vines in
1911, and today it is still very much a family concern.
Your host at the wine tasting will be a member of the family.

The tasting room is basic; there are few trimmings apart
from fascinating old photographs, but visitors are pleasantly
received.

The family owns approximately 100 acres of nonirrigated
vineyards and does all its own processing, aging and bottling.
Special emphasis is given to its red table wines and in particular its Zinfandel (a 100 percent varietal), which has earned
an outstanding local reputation for the winery. Short tours
are available; of special interest are the walls of the original
wine cellar, made from rock quarried in the area. A few old
casks date back to Uhlinger's days.

D'Agostini is a very small winery and therefore has
limited production. Its wine is found mainly in the stores
and restaurants in the Mother Lode area, although bottles
can occasionally be obtained in Sacramento, San Joaquin
county, and in the Bay Area.

*Shenandoah Road, 8 miles northeast of Plymouth;
(209) 245-6612; daily 9 - 5; informal tours.*

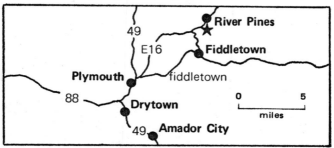

East-Side

The end of the dry Prohibition era led to a resurgence of grape-growing in the Lodi region and the establishment of farmer cooperatives. East-Side is one such organization which was founded in 1934 by 130 local farmers.

The recently constructed tasting room is set among large shade trees a short distance from the main winery buildings. It's designed in the form of an old redwood aging tank (a popular architectural idiom in the wine country) and is appropriately labelled *Das Weinhaus* to reflect the German origins of most of the founders of the cooperative.

Royal Host is the winery's featured brand but its Conti Royal, Gold Bell and Pastene labels are also to be found in different parts of the U. S. East-Side has recently introduced a new wine of which it is especially proud: Angelica Antiqua—Mission 1773. This wine, aged for approximately eight to ten years is made from the first grape variety introduced into California by the Mission fathers sometime between 1769 and 1773. Another unique product is East-Side's Gold wine, made from a grape developed by the researchers at the University of California at Davis.

At the 1972 Los Angeles County Fair, nine of the fourteen products entered by East-Side earned official recognition. In particular, its dry sherry received a Grand Sweepstakes award, the first time in California history that a dessert wine has been so honored.

6100 E. Highway 12, Lodi; (209) 369-4768; daily 9 - 5; guided tours.

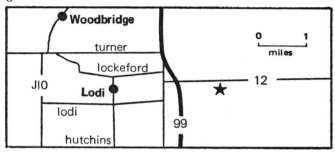

Frasinetti

The Frasinetti tasting room is well hidden between large corrugated iron buildings. Only generic and dessert wines are available and tasting is held in a rather small, restricted area.

The Frasinetti winery began with James Frasinetti in 1897, when he came to California from his native Italy. Frasinetti worked for a while in his uncle's candy factory in San Francisco and later packed grapes during Prohibition before deciding to open his own winery. Choosing the present site, he concentrated on making dinner and dessert wines.

When James Frasinetti died at the age of 91, his sons took over the business. After phylloxera ruined most of their vineyards the brothers started buying all their grapes from other sources. They now blend and bottle all their generic wines, the recommended ones being burgundy, Chablis Blanc and Cerasolo.

Stop by during early August and catch the annual square dance held here. Everyone's invited.

7395 Frasinetti Road, Florin (near Sacramento);
(916) 383-2444; daily 9 - 4; no tours.

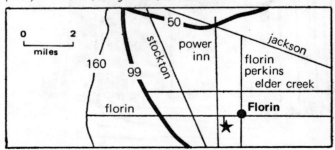

Gold Hill

Here's a story of wine making that started in the kitchen as a hobby, moved to the garage, then to a seven-acre vineyard and finally, in 1968, led to the opening of the Gold Hill Winery. John and Beverly Hempt are the owners of this impressive little concern. John also serves as winemaster.

Gold Hill Winery offers limited quantities of estate-bottled wine. In the past, fruit and berry wines were also available, but no longer. To date, its prized wines are Zinfandel and Johannisberg Riesling. Until recently Gold Hill concentrated on blends, but now the excitement of producing varietals is very evident and plans for Chenin Blanc and Cabernet are under way. Mountain Burgundy, chablis, Coloma Gold, Pink Chablis and burgundy, along with Ruby Port and sherry (the latter two are produced elsewhere) are available for tasting, along with a few treasured varietals.

The wooden tasting room is tiny but cozy. Paintings, sketches, and posters decorate the walls, and a few wine books are for sale.

Highway 49 at Lotus Road, Coloma; (916) 622-1712; Sat. & Sun. 12 - 5, closed weekdays; no tours.

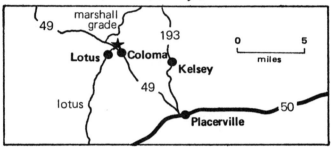

Gibson

Robert Gibson founded the Gibson Wine Company in 1944. After his death in 1960 the winery was sold to the Sanger Corporation, a cooperative of 158 growers. From the old winery, which was originally a gas engine works, the corporation moved its tasting room in 1970 to the present contemporary building which initially was designed as a restaurant.

Gibson had experimented with fruit wines and was a pioneer in the marketing and production of berry wines. Today fresh fruit wines still play a major role in the winery's production. In 1969 it became the first company in the U. S. to produce honey wine (mead). At a recent wine-judging festival, Gibson was presented with a silver medal for its high quality mead. Ironically, the mead which received the gold medal was also prepared by Gibson, but bottled under another winery's label.

Most of the varietals here are produced by another company. Green Hungarian, Barbera and Cabernet are the most outstanding selections. The tasting room is relaxing and extremely well designed. Visitors should welcome the cheese and wafer snacks which help to refresh the palate between wine tastings—a thoughtful little extra. If you feel like lingering awhile, there's a pleasant outdoor picnic area adjoining the tasting room.

Grant Line Road at Highway 99, Elk Grove; (916) 685-9211; daily 10 - 8; no tours.

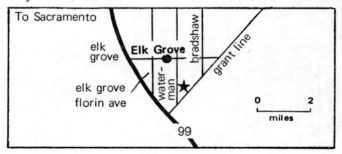

Lockeford

Lockeford Winery's attractive chalet-type tasting room, with its barrel bar, stands alone in a grassy picnic area some distance away from the winery itself. Now owned and operated by the Lockeford Vintner Corporation, the winery was originally constructed in 1946 as a cooperative operation, entirely supported by a local membership of growers. During that time it was a bulk operation with no facilities for bottling its own wines, and until the mid-1960s Lockeford sold most of its wine to other wineries. In 1968 bottling was introduced, along with the production of both still and sparkling wines.

Rhine wine, chablis, sauterne, Zinfandel, French Colombard, (a varietal grape used widely in California champagne and also in France for the production of brandy) and Ruby Cabernet (a varietal grape introduced by researchers at U. C. Davis), along with Lockeford's bulk-processed (Charmat) champagnes, are all sold at the tasting room and available for tasting.

18800 N. Highway 88, Lockeford; (209) 727-5541; daily 10 - 6; tours by appointment.

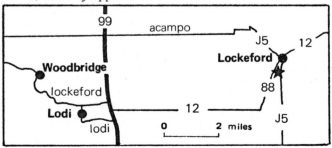

Guild

A friendly greeting from the receptionist, a large, modern tasting room, and a well-displayed selection of wines—these are the visitor's first impressions upon entering the Guild Winery in Lodi. Guild (previously known as the Wine Growers' Guild and, until three years ago, as the Guild Wine Company) is a grower-owned cooperative consisting of approximately 1,000 individual grape growers. Bulk wine is received by the Guild for bottling after it has been produced at seven individual company-owned wineries throughout the state.

At the beginning of the guided tour guests are shown the Winemaster's House, an elegantly furnished restaurant available for private parties. During the summer, concerts are held in the surrounding gardens. A vineyard in front contains 45 different grape varieties, all of which are grown in California—an interesting feature.

Although no actual wine production occurs at the Lodi winery, visitors are shown huge insulated concrete and stainless-steel holding tanks, which contain the bulk wine shipped from the Guild's other wineries. Champagne receives its secondary fermentation here, usually for a period of four to six weeks. In the bottling room, a glass screen separates visitors from the filling machines, and employees on the champagne line wear protective face masks, since there's always a possibility of a champagne bottle blowing its top. In a separate section, endless oak barrels of aging brandy are on display; some are aged for 25 years, others for 50. The brandy aroma is especially memorable.

Guild is the third-largest wine producer in the nation, although most of its production is sold outside California. Tavola, Winemasters, Cresta Blanca, Roma, Ceremony and Cook's Imperial are just a few of the brand names to be found under the aegis of Guild. There's a wide selection of dinner wines for tasting, but the company is particularly well known for its Tavola Red, Gamay Beaujolais, Petite Sirah, Pinot Noir and French Colombard.

1 Winemasters Way, Lodi; (209) 368-5151; daily 10 - 5; guided tours.

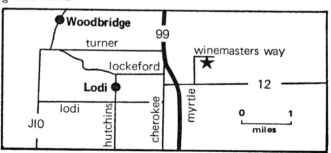

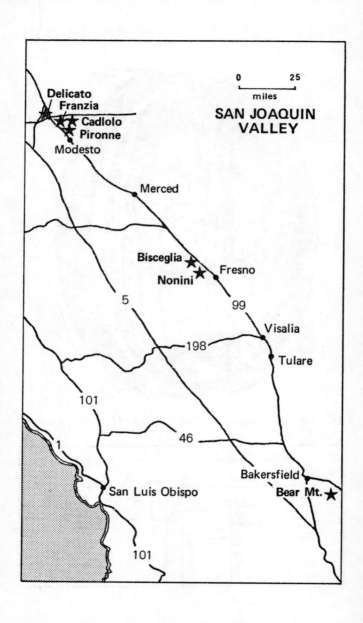

SAN JOAQUIN VALLEY

0   25
miles

Delicato
Franzia
Cadlolo
Pironne
Modesto

Merced

Bisceglia
Nonini
Fresno

5

99

Visalia

198

Tulare

101

46

1

Bakersfield

Bear Mt.

San Luis Obispo

101

Fresno /
San Joaquin
Valley Region

The San Joaquin Valley is one of the most misunderstood of all California's wine regions. In many articles and publications on West Coast wineries, this vast, productive region is given little more than a passing reference. Thus it may be surprising to learn that over 75 percent of California's wine is produced here, and that it is the most rapidly expanding wine production area in the state.

Unfortunately, because of the valley's extreme temperature variations and the composition of its natural soils, grape types grown in the area tend to be limited to varieties used in the production of generic wines. However, changes are imminent. Recent research at the University of California at Davis has led to the development of high-quality grape types in the valley and a subsequent improvement in the standard of locally produced wines. With continued advances in climate control and "genetic engineering," the area's contribution to premium wine production may well increase significantly.

The San Joaquin Valley contains an unusual collection of wineries. On the one hand are huge corporations such as Bear Mountain (M. LaMont label), Franzia and Gallo (not open to the public). Among them they account for a mammoth proportion of the state's wine production. Then there are the smaller establishments with unfamiliar names, such as Bisceglia, Cadlolo, Nonini and Pirrone, all of which produce limited selections of primarily generic wines. Try to visit these places if you can. You may be surprised by the quality of their products.

Bear Mountain

Bear Mountain Winery, the largest shipper of California bulk wines to the bottling trade, was formed in 1966 as a growers cooperative. At that time a group of growers purchased the Di Giorgio winery facilities, originally used for production of dessert wines. Since then Bear Mountain has instituted many improvements and modernizations to the winery primarily to expand production to include table wines.

The first packaged Bear Mountain wines were marketed in 1970. However, in August 1972, the new M. LaMont label was introduced which today includes a complete line of premium varietal wines: Emerald Riesling, French Colombard, Chenin Blanc, Grenache Rosé, Cabernet, Semillon, Zinfandel and Barbera. The generic wines bottled under this new label contain at least 51 percent of the quality varietal grapes named on the label. Gold Peak, Pinos Mountain and Mountain Gold are other Bear Mountain labels, but its focus appears to be on the M. LaMont brand wines and on a continued expansion of premium wines.

Bear Mountain has two wine-tasting rooms, one located at the winery and another at the Colony Kitchen Restaurant off Highway 99, four miles south of Bakersfield. If you can spare the time for a side trip and the 45-minute tour, the winery itself is well worth a visit.

Comanche Drive and Di Giorgio Road, Lamont;
(805) 845-2231; weekdays 10 - 5, weekends 11 - 6;
guided tours.

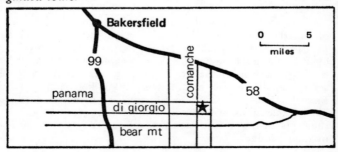

Bisceglia Brothers

For some reason, the road signs directing visitors to this winery read "California Wine Tasting Rooms"—there is no evidence of the name Bisceglia. The company has only one tasting room.

The Bisceglias, once active vintners in Calabria, Italy, began their California wine making in 1888. In 1952, Alfonse Bisceglia, the last of the original founders, passed away, and since that time the winery has been managed by Joseph, Bruno and Bruno, Jr.

The winery buys and produces wine for blending. It is therefore in a position to offer a vast range of wines, although it leans toward the generics. Chateau D'or and Chateau Rouge are considered to be two of the Bisceglias' most interesting wines. The tasting selection is wide and includes white, rosé and red table wines as well as sparkling, dessert, fruit and berry wines. Paradise, once the company's leading brand, was discontinued in 1965. Today its own wines, labeled under Imperial Vintners, Golden Chalice and Bisceglia, are available only at the winery.

25427 Avenue 13, Madera; (209) 673-3594; daily 9 - 5; no tours.

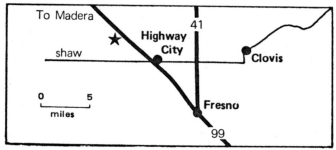

Cadlolo

Recalling their activities during the grape-crushing season, Ray Cadlolo describes himself and his brother, Theodore, as "two fellows running around like chickens with their heads cut off!" The brothers have run the Cadlolo Winery single-handedly since their father, Charles, handed it over to them in 1955. The main building dates back to 1913, when Charles Cadlolo's uncle, Louis Sciaroni, built the winery and the adjoining family home.

Ray and Theodore Cadlolo buy all their grapes, but crushing is done at the winery through September and mid-October. (Onlookers are invited, providing that they keep out of the way.) Much of their wine is processed in bulk and shipped to some of the better-known establishments in the Napa and Sonoma regions (precisely which ones is a well-kept secret).

One of the brothers will provide an informal and chatty tour, during which visitors will be shown the grape crusher

(a superb piece of equipment), the old open concrete fermenting tanks, the storage area and the hand-operated bottling and labeling facilities, (better known as the "armstrong machinery"). Tasting is offered from a selection of mainly dry wines. The winery's burgundy and Mellow Red are particularly recommended.

1124 California Street, Escalon; (209) 838-2457; daily, except Sun. 8 - 5; informal tours.

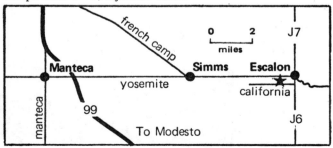

Delicato

Wanting to abandon the name Sam-Jasper, by which most of its wines have been known, and deciding that the family name was not the most appropriate of names for a new winery, the Indelicato clan recently selected the Delicato label for its new wines. This small winery, now run by three brothers and their families, dates back to 1935 when it was founded by Sebastiano Luppino and Gaspare Indelicato. (Sebastiano's nickname was Sam, and Gaspare was known as Jasper—hence the origin of the earlier label.)

The Indelicatos sell some of their products to other wineries besides providing a considerable selection of their own dry wines: burgundy, Zinfandel, claret, chianti, Grenache Rosé and Chablis Blanc, to name a few. Their popular new line, Tingle—a lemon-flavored white wine and a fruit-flavored pink—was introduced in the early 1960s.

The present tasting room at Delicato Cellars is tiny, and the noisy bottling plant is right next door. The family hopes to build a new tasting room on the premises in the near future.

12001 South Highway 99, 4 miles north of Manteca; (209) 823-5616; daily 9 - 5; tours by appointment only.

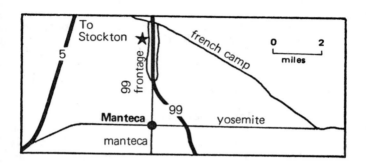

Franzia

The Franzia Brothers Winery, one of the largest producing wineries in California, is now a public corporation, but it continues to be operated by the Franzia brothers. Their father, Giuseppe Franzia, who came from Italy in the early 1900s, purchased the ranch in 1906. Giuseppe started his business by selling grapes, and in 1915 produced his first wines. In 1933 his five sons, the present managers, entered the business. During that year they produced 100,000 gallons of wine. Today, they claim the capacity to produce 8 million gallons a year.

The winery is very much a businesslike concern. The only remaining family touches are the photographs of the founder and his wife displayed in the modern tasting room, where visitors are graciously received.

Zinfandel, Grenache, Carignane and champagne (prepared by the Charmat process) are just a sampling from Franzia's extensive range of red and white dinner wines and sparkling, appetizer and dessert wines. There's an open picnic area in front of the tasting room for visitors who feel like staying awhile.

6 miles E. of Manteca on Highway 120, Ripon; (209) 559-4251; 10 - 6 Oct. - May, 10 - 8 June - Sept.; no tours.

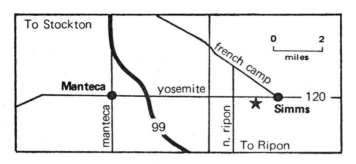

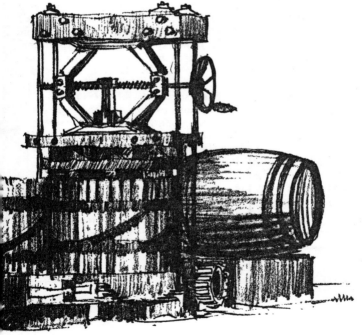

Nonini

A thorough hour-and-a-half tour, a pour-your-own-wine policy and a warm welcome by one of the three Nonini brothers are unusual features at the family-owned A. Nonini Winery.

The Noninis are rapidly extending their range of wines, and hope to soon release Barbera, Zinfandel Rosé, Chablis Blanc and Zinfandel under a new label, A. Nonini Premium. By 1974 they plan to introduce two more wines, Grenache and claret. Their currently recommended selections include vin rosé, Sweet Zinfandel and Chablis Blanc, all produced from their own vineyard.

The vine-clad bell from a school the brothers once attended occupies a prominent position near the tasting room, evidence of the family's sentimental attachment to the area. The Noninis have lived at the winery since 1936, when its founder, Antonio Nonini—who had arrived from Northern Italy with only $10 to his name and struggled through many hard years of farming in the valley—was finally able to create a successful winery for his sons.

2640 North Dickenson Avenue, Fresno; (209) 264-7857; Mon. - Sat. 8 - 6, Sun. 10 - 4; tours by appointment.

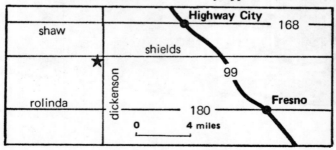

Pironne

The tasting room at the Pirrone Wine Cellars in Salida is the only place where Pirrone wines can be purchased. It's a modern, neatly laid-out facility, designed by Frank Pirrone (who was originally an architect) when he bought the winery in 1936. Frank Pirrone had acquired some California vineyards in the mid-1920s, and for sometime commuted back and forth from New Jersey, harvesting grapes for his personal use. When he finally settled in California, he extended his production and began to sell his wines to other companies.

The winery has since passed to Frank's son, Alfred (a graduate of U. C. Davis) and Alfred's wife, Lois. The majority of Pirrone wines continue to be sold to other wineries, but there's an impressive range of selections available for tasting on the premises: white dinner wines (Johannisberg Riesling, Chenin Blanc, Green Hungarian), red dinner wines (burgundy, Cabernet Sauvignon, Barbera, Pinot Noir, Zinfandel) and a few dry and cream sherries. Champagnes, fruit and berry wines are also available, but these are not produced by the winery.

5258 Pirrone Road, Salida; (209) 545-0704; daily 9 - 5; tours daily at 10 & 2 during Sept. and Oct.

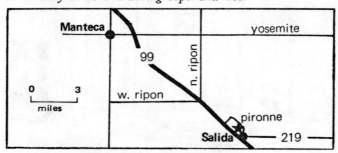

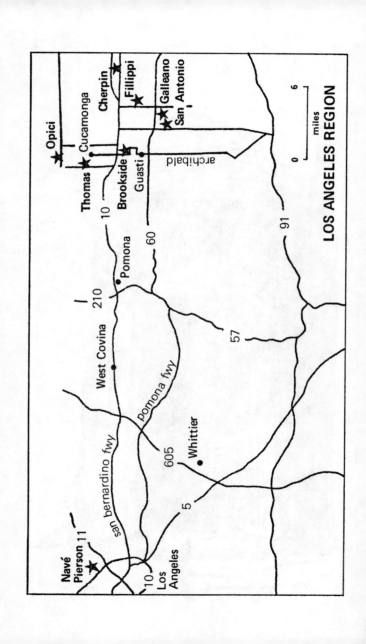

LOS ANGELES REGION

Cucamonga /
Los Angeles Region

It's hard to believe that the Union Station in downtown Los Angeles stands on what used to be a flourishing vineyard, or that the suburban tracts of Anaheim sprawl across land that was once owned by an exclusive German colony renowned for its fine wine production.

During the early 1800s, the Los Angeles area produced two-thirds of all California wines. Unfortunately, the combination of phylloxera, which has plagued vine-growing areas throughout the world, Prohibition and an insatiable demand for housing land has swept away most reminders of those early days of Southern California wine production.

Fortunately the area still contains a few hardy wineries that are waging a lonely but determined battle against urban sprawl and pollution. It even boasts a new addition, the Navé Pierson Winery, which was established in 1970 on San Fernando Road in Los Angeles. Other significant wine names around Southern California include Brookside (headquarters of a statewide system of tasting-room and retail sales outlets), Opici (with vineyards in the Sonoma Valley). Filippi, Cherpin, San Antonio, Galleano and Thomas, the oldest producing winery in California. How long these wineries can continue to exist productively is anybody's guess, but we suggest you visit them as soon as possible.

Brookside

Theophile Vache, who was planting vineyards in Monterey County as early as 1832, was the man responsible for initiating the Brookside Vineyard Company's long and impressive history. Members of the Vache family began making wines in Southern California in 1883. In 1892 they hired Marius Biane a young French immigrant who later courted and married Marcelline, one of the Vache daughters. Subsequent generations of Bianes remained in the wine business, and in 1956 the family established Brookside at its present location in Guasti.

The Bianes remained sole owners until the spring of 1973, when the company was merged with Beatrice Foods, of Chicago. We are told that the Bianes will continue to run things as before, but that now there is a little more money available for future plans and improvements, including the development of new vineyards in the Temecula area of Riverside County.

Surprising as it may seem, Brookside wines can be purchased only at its sales cellars. However, since the winery
has thirty tasting rooms (two of which are in Arizona), most
Californians are within driving distance of Brookside's
popular sherries and table wines. In addition to its original
Southern California outlets, Brookside took over 12
tasting rooms in Northern California when it purchased
the Mills Winery in 1969. For a full list, write to the main
winery in Guasti.

The tours at the Guasti winery can be fun, especially
since they are self-conducted. A visitor is handed a pamphlet
describing individual segments of the tour, pointed in the
right direction and told "go!" Tours encompass the flor
sherry aging room, a specially-laid-out wine museum, an
underground aging cellar, ground-level aging and finishing
cellars, and the bottling plant.

Brookside's wine list contains more than 100 selections
of red and white dinner wines, sparkling wines, sherries, etc.,
in addition to cooking wine, vinegars, Tahiti Joe mixes and
wine jellies, plus a wide range of wines under the Assumption
Abbey label. The Brookside flor sherries are considered outstanding.

9900 "A" Street, Guasti; (714) 986-9377; daily 10 - 7;
self-conducted tours on weekdays, guides available on weekends.

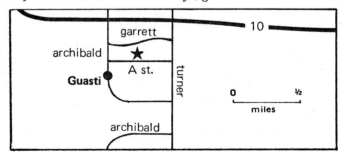

Louis Cherpin

On the dirt path leading up to the Louis Cherpin winery, visitors are more than likely to be greeted by both a yelping dog and a member of the Cherpin family who will run out to open the tasting room door. A poster created by the Cherpin children depicts two seated ladies sharing a bottle of wine and reads "Share it with a friend." It is a family winery dating back to 1922, when Louis Cherpin brought his new bride, **Augustine**, to California to celebrate their honeymoon. The return trip home to France never materialized. Instead, they remained in California to grow grapes.

The winery has since passed to Louis's sons, Eugene, Joe and Leon. If you're interested in a tour, just ask: providing that they have time, the brothers are happy to show visitors around. Joe, our host, looked as though he had just spent a full day in the vineyard.

Burgundy is the Cherpins' most popular wine, closely followed by rosé and Zinfandel. Port, muscatel, vermouth, sauterne and claret are samplings of the remaining stock. Much of the family's current 60,000-gallon annual production is issued under local restaurant labels.

15567 Valley Boulevard, Fontana; (714) 822-4103; daily 8 - 5; guided tours upon request.

Filippi

The extensive range of wines listed in the catalog of the Joseph Filippi Vineyard Company may, at first glance, seem confusing. The Filippi family, however, is attempting to cater to different tastes and different price ranges. It's Pride of Cucamonga and Pride of California are limited lines of young red and white table wines including burgundy, sauterne, vin rosé and Vino Rosso. Chateau Filippi is claimed to be an above-average line of wines prepared from good-quality grapes and aged somewhat longer. The winery's Vino Rosso, Light Sweet Muscat, tokay, Ruby Port, White Port and Black Muscat, along with three sherries, all received high awards at the 1972 Los Angeles County Fair. The

Joseph Filippi label is used only for its premium varietal wines—Gewürztraminer, Barbera, Johannisberg Riesling and Cabernet—and its premium champagne and sparkling wines.

In 1965 the family corporation, headed by Joe Filippi, opened five additional tasting rooms in Southern California and plans to add a sixth in the near future. In 1967 the Filippis purchased the Thomas Vineyards, said to be the oldest operating winery in California.

Etiwanda Avenue at Jurupa, South Fontana; (714) 984-4514; daily 8 - 6; no tours.

Galleano

An incredible number of local people consider this "their" winery. The tasting room is very small, but Mary Galleano (who came from working with chickens to blending wines), bustles around smiling, chatting and trying to find boxes and paper bags to hold the numerous bottles of wines she sells daily.

The winery has been in action since 1933, when it was founded by Domenic Galleano. Today, it still remains a family corporation with Domenic's son, Bernard, as the winemaster.

The Galleanos produce reasonably priced burgundies, Zinfandels, rosés, sauternes, ports, sherries, muscatel, and champagnes. The setting of this interesting winery is informal and rather farmlike, compared to most others. As the only producing winery in Riverside County, it is worth visiting.

4231 Wineville Road, Mira Loma; (714) 685-5376; daily, except Sun. 8 - 6; no tours.

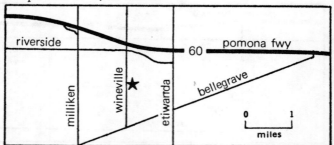

Opici

Unless you live in New York or New Jersey, where Hubert Opici distributes his Opici-label wines, you won't get to sample them without a visit to his tasting room in Alta Loma. Be prepared for prices a little higher than normal for the Cucamonga area.

From the outside, the square, somewhat anonymous building of the Opici Winery is not especially inviting, but inside is an attractive visitor-oriented tasting room where wine and cookbooks, elegant glassware, ornate candles and jars of preserves, teas and spices are on display in fresh, white-walled surroundings.

Joseph Opici began making wine in California in the early 1900s. After his death in 1962, the winery became a family owned corporation headed by his daughter, Mary Opici Nimmergut. Since the winery itself is in the Sonoma Valley, there are no tours in Alta Loma; but visitors are encouraged to taste.

Opici offers a fair range of imported Italian and French wines in addition to San Martin fruit wines, which are considered exceptional. In a class of their own, however, are the Opici premium wines: Chenin Blanc, Pinot Chardonnay, Gewürztraminer, Johannisberg Riesling and Cabernet Sauvignon.

Highland and Hermosa Avenues, Alta Loma; (714) 987-2710; daily, except Tues. & Wed. 10 - 6; no tours.

Navé Pierson

The Sterling Groves orchards in Fallbrook, California share honors for your delight in this fruity-flavored, bright-eyed selection. Their crops consistently produce the finest purple stock available, and the result will be unmistakable. Saint Rose herself would bless the end result of Navé Pierson's prayerful attention to the Santa Rosa plum. (P.S. to ice cream advocates: Plummet into a taste adventure—get the scoop, then pour it on!) Serve chilled.

Produced and Bottled by Navé Pierson Winery Los Angeles, California

Sam Pierson and Les Navé founded their winery in 1970—the first to be established in the city of Los Angeles since 1917. Now they have two locations, although the second, in Playa del Rey, is a tasting room only.

Starting out in the back yard of his South Pasadena home, Sam Pierson produced wine, purely as a hobby, for the enjoyment of his family and friends. When he reached the point where demand grossly exceeded his output, he gave up his spare-time attempts at domestic production and started his own fully equipped winery—complete with Southern California's only rotary vacuum filter, which can process 4,000 gallons a day.

Navé Pierson produces 22 different varieties of wine. It's chablis, sauterne and Chenin Blanc won high recognition at the Los Angeles County Fair in 1972. The winery is particulary proud of its burgundy, Zinfandel, Barbera, Mountain Rosé, Zinfandel Rosé rhine wine, May wine and its famous apricot, plum and strawberry fruit wines. Both the San Fernando Road winery and the Playa del Rey tasting room have snack bars that sell delicious sandwiches, salads and cheeses.

1204 San Fernando Road, Los Angeles; (213) 221-2114; daily 8 - 8; informal tours. Tasting room: 337 Culver Boulevard, Playa del Rey; (213) 821-7177; daily 10 - 9; Sun. 10 - 6; no tours.

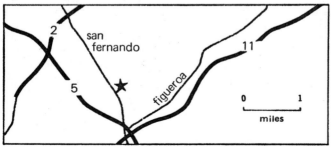

San Antonio

If you're out searching for the Countyline Wine Cellars in Ontario, forget it; that establishment closed down a couple of years ago. In its place, however, and apparently thriving, is one of the San Antonio Winery tasting rooms. From the outside it is a hodgepodge affair of pink and red roofs, with a tiny rock fountain pool (terrific for duck-sized waders), an old bulging wine-barrel wagon and masses of vines, ivy and other greenery. The tasting room is bright and cheerful, with rows of San Antonio wines, glassware, books, bright-colored table arrangements and arched display areas.

The wine list is endless. Fruit wines are offered (apricot, plum and pear were recently added to the line), in addition to champagne, and such specialties as Almondoro, Marsalovo and Cardinale, French imported wines, premium wines including Cabernet Sauvignon, Pinot Chardonnay and Barbera, dessert wines and Italian-type wines.

Tours are offered only at the main producing winery in Los Angeles. But if you're looking for a pleasant tasting room in a rural pocket of the sprawling Greater Los Angeles area, this is the place to come.

12747 Milliken Avenue, Ontario; (714) 986-8286; daily, except Mon. 10 - 7; no tours. Tours given at main winery, 737 Lamar Street, Los Angeles.

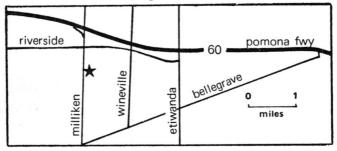

Thomas

The Thomas Vineyards, reported to be the oldest producing winery in California, was originally known as the Cucamonga Rancho winery. It was founded by Tiburcio Tapis after he received a land grant from Governor Juan Bautista Alvarado of Mexico in March, 1839. The winery was sold to the Joseph Filippi Vineyard Co. in 1967, but two years later a ruinous flood swept through the area, destroying much of its stock and some of the original winery buildings. As a result, wines are now produced at the Filippi winery, with a portion of the aging being carried out at the Thomas facilities.

Visitors who take the winery's self-conducted tour will discover an unusual little museum in the back yard, where a Lancia Lamda car and a Stutz fire engine, both dated 1924, are displayed in venerable splendor. There's also a 61,783-gallon tank that has been opened to enable visitors to take a walk inside (where they are likely to find that inhaling wine

fumes can be almost as intoxicating as drinking the stuff). Close by there's a tiny picnic area.

The selection of wines offered for sampling is impressive and includes the vineyard's dinner and fruit wines, along with premium wines such as Barbera, Pinot Noir and Riesling.

8916 Foothill Boulevard, Cucamonga; (714) 987-1612; daily 8 - 6; informal tours.

Other Wineries

The following wineries are open to the public by appointment only.

DAVID BRUCE

David Bruce, a San Jose physician, offers tasting and tours at his winery on Saturdays by appointment only. It it a rapidly growing concern. Dr. Bruce specializes in Pinot Noir, Chardonnay, Zinfandel, Cabernet Sauvignon and White Riesling, plus a Zinfandel White.

21439 Bear Creek Road, Los Gatos 95030; (408) 354-4214.

BURGESS

For the best view in the Napa Valley, Burgess Cellars is the winery to visit. There are no tastings, but visitors are more than welcome to inspect rosé, chablis, Chenin Blanc or rhine wine, or simply admire the scenery. Premium red varietals will become available in 1975.

1108 Deer Park Road, St. Helena 94574; (707) 963-4766.

BUTLER

The Butlers had just expanded their winery when a disastrous fire destroyed the entire complex and all their wine stock. The Butler Winery specialized in two wines, Wild Elderberry, made from berries picked from the surrounding area, and Alecante Bouschet, made from the locally grown Alecante grapes. All its wines are made without filtering and aged in 50-gallon casks. Roger Butler is hoping to reopen in January, 1974. We wish him better luck.

Route 3, Box 357, Longeway Road, Sonora 95370; (209) 532-6183.

CALIFORNIA GROWERS

There is no tasting at this winery, but tours are given—preferably by appointment. The retail room displays a full line of dessert and table wines along with champagne, brandy and a wide selection of flavored wines. California Growers Wineries is a grower cooperative that dates back to 1934.

P. O. Box 38, 38558 Road 128, Cutler 93615;
(209) 528-3055.

CHALONE

The small Chalone Vineyard, next to the Pinnacles National Monument, produces only varietals: Pinot Noir, Pinot Blanc, Chenin Blanc and Chardonnay. It is a winery with a very limited production; consequently, write ahead to request tours.

P. O. Box 855, Soledad 93960.

CHATEAU MONTELENA

This winery is temporarily closed to visitors because it is currently out of stock. It should be opening again in a year or two, so watch for news.

1429 Tubbs Lane, Calistoga 94515; (707) 942-4060.

FICKLIN

The very small Ficklin Vineyards devotes almost all its energy to the production of one wine, Ficklin Port. Small lots of Emerald Riesling and Ruby Cabernet are also produced. The winery was founded in 1948 and its first wines were released in 1952. It is a family-run operation, and tours and tasting are not encouraged.

30246 Avenue 7½, Madera 93637; (209) 674-4598.

FOPPIANO

The L. Foppiano Wine Company currently boasts outstanding Zinfandel, Cabernet Sauvignon, Pinot Noir and Petite Sirah varietals. The land it occupies was purchased in 1896 by John Foppiano. Today Louis Foppiano and his family carry on the wine making tradition. The winery is open daily from 10 to 4, and tours can be arranged by appointment.

12700 Old Redwood Highway, Healdsburg 95448; (707) 433-1937.

FREEMARK ABBEY

This winery is open to the public daily for retail sales and on-the-hour tours, but prior appointments are needed for tasting. Johannisberg Riesling, Chardonnay, Pinot Noir and Cabernet Sauvignon can be purchased here. It's a pleasant place to visit, and the adjoining Hurd candle shop is an extra bonus.

3022 St. Helena Highway North, P. O. Box 410, St. Helena 94574; (707) 963-7105.

GEMELLO

The Gemello Winery offers tasting by appointment only, but its retail sales office, located on the premises, is open daily. Gemello specializes in Cabernet Sauvignon and Zinfandel.

2003 El Camino Real, Mountain View 94040; (415) 948-7723.

HANZELL

The Hanzell Vineyards had sold all its stock when we stopped by. Fresh supplies of two wines, Pinot Noir and Chardonnay, were scheduled to be released by September or October, 1973. It is a small winery, and tours are by appointment only.

18596 Lomita Avenue, Sonoma 95476; (707) 996-3860.

LLORDS & ELWOOD

Mike Elwood has been involved in the wine industry since 1933. The family owned a chain of retail stores throughout Hollywood, Beverly Hills and Brentwood in which the world's most famous wines were sold. In 1961 the Elwoods decided to try their own luck in the wine making business, specializing in sherries and champagne, and have since achieved much success. They currently produce a total of ten varieties including fine table wines.

P. O. Box 3397, Fremont 94538.

MAYACAMAS

Mayacamas Vineyards is a beautifully situated winery, offering magnificent views of the surrounding countryside. Appointments are essential for tours; no tasting is offered. The present owners, Bob and Noni Travers, bought the winery in 1968 and now produce primarily Chardonnay and Cabernet Sauvignon.

1155 Lokoya Road, Napa 94558; (707) 224-4030.

F. J. MILLER

Although appointments are essential, a visit to F. Justin Miller's residence and winery is a definite must for people who are intensely interested in wines and wine making procedures. This 70-year-old Englishman, who is considered too unconventional by many elitists of the wine world, is surely one of the most controversial figures in the industry today. The cause of the controversy is his patented Miller-way process, which is a method of converting still wine into sparkling wine in a matter of hours. Miller's process seems quite logical, and he explains everything in a clear, matter-of-fact manner to his many fascinated visitors.

8329 St. Helena Highway, Napa 94558; (707) 963-4252.

NERVO

The Nervo Winery, a family enterprise that concentrates primarily on the production of wine for other wineries, offers a 1944 Zinfandel, a Pinot St. George, and two unusual selections, Malvoise and Beclan Cabernet, along with burgundy, Zinfandel, sauterne and Chenin Blanc. Its wines can only be bought, or sampled in small paper cups, at the simple tasting room, which is open from 9 to 5 daily. The family prefers that visitors make appointments for tastings.

19585 Redwood Highway South, Geyserville 95441; (707) 857-9902.

NICASIO

Dan Wheeler named his winery Nicasio Vineyards after the Indian word meaning "beautiful hidden valley." He has been making wine on a commercial basis for the past 20 years. Although he was the first member of the family to enter the field, he has developed an impressive line of un-filtered premium varietals including Johannisberg Riesling, Chardonnay, Zinfandel Rosé, Zinfandel and Cabernet Sauvignon. In addition he produces a natural champagne, which is very dry with no *dosage* added.

Tours and tasting are given only on Sundays by appointment, and it is wise to give two to three weeks' notice.

14300 Nicasio Way, Soquel 95073; (408) 423-1073.

MARTIN RAY

Martin Ray produces four premium varietal wines: Pinot Noir, Cabernet Sauvignon, Chardonnay and White Riesling. An occasional bottle of his wine can sell for as high as $50. Written requests for appointments are necessary for both tasting and tours.

22000 Mt. Eden Road, Saratoga 95070.

RIDGE

If you visit the Ridge Vineyards without prior appointment, preferably arranged for a time between noon and 3 on Saturday afternoons, you will probably find that no one is free to welcome you. The view from this winery is truly spectacular, although it is a long drive from the main highway.

Four main varietals are produced here: Cabernet Sauvignon, Zinfandel, Petite Sirah and Chardonnay. The winery is having problems meeting the unprecedented customer demand for Ridge wines, but it is trying.

17100 Monte Bello Road Cupertino, 95014; (408) 867-3233.

SCHRAMSBERG

The burdens associated with fame and renown have recently fallen upon this impressive little winery. Its problems began when President Nixon took along a selection of its four champagnes on his visit to Peking, thereby thrusting the Schramsberg Vineyards into international prominence.

There is no tasting because production is limited, but tours are available by prior appointment.

Schramsberg Road, Highway 29, Calistoga 94515;
(707) 942-4558

SPRING MOUNTAIN

This three-wine enterprise (Pinot Chardonnay, Cabernet Sauvignon and Sauvignon Blanc) is owned by Michael and Shirley Robbins. Although Spring Mountain Vineyards, is small concern, its first releases have proved to be extremely successful. Because production is limited, there is no tasting, but tours can be arranged preferably by appointment.

2867 St. Helena Highway North, St. Helena 95474.
(707) 963-4341.

STONY HILL

A mountain-terraced vineyard of 28 acres and a production of three white 100-percent varietal wines—Chardonnay, Gewürztraminer and Johannisberg Riesling—are the proud possessions of Eleanor and Fred McCrea. By word of mouth, the Stony Hill Vineyard has built an impressive following, but due to limited production its wines are sold only by mail or at the winery. Visits can be arranged by appointment.

P. O. Box 308, St. Helena 94574; (707) 963-2636.

New Tasting Rooms

The following wineries have only recently opened to the public, but each is worth a visit.

CRESTA BLANCA

With deep roots in California's Livermore Valley dating back to 1883, the Cresta Blanca winery has recently entered a new era: its ownership has changed (it is now one of the Guild wineries), its location has been changed and its packaging has been completely redesigned.

The former Mendocino Vineyards winery in Ukiah has become the Cresta Blanca home winery, utilizing vineyard yields from the Mendocino, Sonoma and Napa regions. A complete selection of varietal wines is available to visitors in the tasting room, which is open from 10 to 5 daily.

2399 North State Street, Ukiah 95482; (707) 462-0565

CUVAISON

This winery is open every weekend from 11 to 5 for tours and tasting, and on weekdays by appointment. It is a new winery, founded in the spring of 1971, with Tom Cottrell as owner, wine maker and president. To date he has three wines: Chenin Blanc, Chardonnay, and Gamay Vivace. A fourth, 1972 Sauvignon Blanc, is soon to be released, and a 1971 Cabernet Sauvignon is quietly resting in Limousin barrels.

4560 Silverado Trail, Calistoga 94515; (707) 942-6100.

DRY CREEK

Dry Creek Vineyard is Sonoma County's newest premium quality winery. It was founded by David Stare, who moved to California from New England in 1971. Wine production was begun in leased space in 1972, and three 100 percent varietal wines were produced: Chenin Blanc, Fume Blanc, and Chardonnay, which is still aging in French barrels. Dry Creek's own modest winery, under construction in the beautiful Dry Creek Valley, will be completed for the 1973 harvest. At that time the winery planned to begin producing red wines, including Zinfandel and Cabernet Sauvignon, in addition to its continued output of a limited selection of whites.

3770 Lambert Bridge Road, Healdsburg 95448; (707) 433-1000.

EDMEADES

Most Edmeades wines are still aging, but in the summer of 1973 French Colombard, Pinot Chardonnay and Gewürztraminer will be offered for tasting. By the summer of 1974, Cabernet Sauvignon and Zinfandel should also be available. For current information, write to the winery.

5500 State Highway 128, Philo 95466.

FETZER

This small winery founded by Bernard Fetzer is truly a family concern. The Fetzers have 11 children, and each plays a role in helping run the winery. Their first wines were released in 1970; today the selection consists of Cabernet Sauvignon, Zinfandel, Pinot Noir, Blanc de Blanc and Gamay Beaujolais. All wines are vintage-dated and most are estate-bottled. Both tours and tasting are offered, but by appointment only.

1150 Bel Arbres Road, Redwood Valley 95470;
(707) 485-8671.

FRANCISCAN

This is yet another new winery to be built in contemporary California Mission style. It is due to open in late

1973, but tasting will not begin until the spring of 1974. Present plans call for the production of primarily varietal wines.

1178 Galleron Road, Rutherford 94573; (707) 963-3886.

HUSCH

Gretchen and Tony Husch moved to Mendocino County several years ago to escape what they describe as "urban fatigue." Their winery has a small production of 100 percent varietals and offers very limited tasting. They are extremely proud of their Pinot Chardonnay, Pinot Noir, Cabernet Sauvignon and Gewürztraminer.

P. O. Box 144, Philo 95466; (707) 895-3216.

MATHEWS

At the main office in Newport Beach, the Mathews Winery maintains an informal tasting room, which is open Monday through Friday from 10 to 5. During the summer of 1973, the family intends to offer tastings in its Napa winery, at 1711 Main Street in Napa. Pinot Noir, Chenin Blanc and Gamay stand out as being exceptional. Tastings are held at the Newport Beach location on weekends by appointment only.

4540 Campus Drive, P. O. Box 1042, Newport Beach 92663; (714) 540-2266.

ROMA

Roma is part of the Guild cooperative. Although a relatively old winery, it has a new tasting room of contemporary design which opened in Fresno in June, 1973. An impressive brandy-still complex will play a major role in the winery's future production, and a full range of sparkling table wines is available for tasting from 10 to 5 daily. Tours are also offered.

3223 East Church Avenue, Fresno 93714; (209) 485-3080.

SANTA BARBARA

Recently remodeled, this tasting room and winery is among the smallest in California. Its Solvang fruit wines, made by that town's Danish inhabitants from .traditional recipes, are its best sellers to date; but the winery is becoming increasingly proud of its chablis, vin rosé, Sauvignon Blanc and burgundy. This is a totally informal place and well worth a visit to enjoy a glass of wine and an informal tour of the winery (10 - 5:30 daily).

202 Anacapa Street, Santa Barbara 93108; (805) 966-5012.

TRENTADUE

This new winery, which was expected to be completed during the summer of 1973, is owned by Leo Trentadue and his charming wife, Evelyn. In 1972 Leo produced 10,000 gallons of wines and his goal is to reach 25,000. Their wines to date include Early Burgundy, Petite Sirah, Cabernet Sauvignon, Zinfandel, Chenin Blanc, Semillon and Carignane. Most of their varietals contain 100 percent of the named grapes, all from their own 150-acre vineyard. Wines are aged mostly in 50-gallon oak barrels, and no artifical means of clarification is used. Tastings are offered daily from 10 to 5.

19170 Redwood Highway, Geyserville 95441; (707) 433-3104.

ZD WINERY

This two-family winery, owned and managed by Norman de Leuze and Gino R. Zepponi, produced its first crush in 1969. Although now offering four wines—Pinot Noir, Chardonnay, White Riesling and Gewürztraminer, all 100 percent varietals—the families plan to specialize in the first two. Expansion is likely but this will be limited in order to maintain the current high standards of premium wines. Tours are available only by special appointment.

Box 900, Sonoma 95476; (707) 539-9137.

Reading a California Wine Label

Estate Bottled — Varies in significance, depending on the size and caliber of the winery. Officially it defines a wine produced entirely from grapes grown in vineyards owned or controlled by the winery.

Name of the wine company — This is the name of the winery which *markets* the product. Unless stated specifically on the label, the wine is not necessarily produced at that winery.

Name of the wine — Wines are named in one of three ways: generic, varietal or proprietary. Generic wines either have broad categorical names (e.g., chianti, vin rosé) or are after European wine-providing regions (e.g., burgundy, moselle, rhine). There are no legal limitations on the use of these names nor recommendations for the composition of the wine. Varietal wines are named after the predominant grape varietal used to produce the wine. At least 51 percent of the wine must be made from the named grape. Proprietary or trademarked names are owned by the wineries and are used only for specific wines (e.g., Emerald Dry, Chateau la Salle, Ripple).

Vintage date — Appearing more regularly on wine labels, a vintage date indicates that 100 percent of the wine contained in the bottle was produced from grapes harvested that particular year.

Produced and Bottled by . . . — Indicates that 75 percent of the wine was crushed, aged and finished by the named winery.

Made and Bottled by . . . — At least 10 percent of the wine must have been produced at the named winery.

Bottled by . . ., Cellared by . . ., Perfected by . . ., etc. — Indicates that the named winery merely finished and bottled the wine.

Alcoholic content — White table wine must contain, legally, between 10 and 14 percent alcohol and red wine, between 10.5 and 14 percent.

Private Stock — Somewhat ambiguous. Any winery can describe its wines by this term. However, at most wineries it denotes specially selected high-quality wine. The same comment applies to such descriptions as *Limited Bottling* and *Private Reserve,* as well as numbered·labels and cask or cuvee numbers.

Back labels — Many wineries are abandoning the old practice of using back labels as romantic advertising copy and, instead, are providing concise descriptions of the contents and production methods applicable to the bottled wine.

ESTATE BOTTLED

Grand Cru Vineyards
Sonoma Valley
ZINFANDEL
BLANC de NOIR
1971
PRODUCED AND BOTTLED BY GRAND CRU VINEYARDS, INC.
GLEN ELLEN, CALIFORNIA
ALCOHOL 12.5% BY VOLUME

Glossary

Astringency
Related to the tannin content in the wine. Although a certain amount is desirable, an excessive amount of tannin produces a sharpness or tartness which causes the mouth to pucker.

Binning
The storing of newly bottled wine before it is released to the retailer or consumer. Some red varietals may receive several years of binning before reaching their primes. A longer period of binning is the optional responsibility of the consumer. Wines sold at retail are often relatively young, although they may be ready to drink for those who enjoy the fruity characteristics of youth.

Bonded Winery
A winery that has a legal permit for producing and storing wines and which also allows tasting on its premises.

Brut
Usually refers to sparkling wines like champagne and means *dry*, although the wine may have a very slight sweetness.

Candling
The procedure of holding a bottle of wine against a lit candle to check its clarity.

Carbonated Wine
A wine made "sparkling" by the injection of carbon dioxide gas.

Champagne
A sparkling wine produced by a second fermentation in closed tanks, which results in the wine's retention of carbon dioxide. When a bottle of champagne is opened, the gas is released and bubbles are seen.

Champenoise Process The traditional French process for champagne making. After the still wines are blended and sugar and yeast are added, the wine is then bottled and undergoes a second fermentation that takes two to three years. The sediment which forms is then worked into the neck of the bottle. The neck is then frozen, the top is removed and the sediment is disgorged. A blend of wine and sugar (the *dosage*) is added to replace wine lost in disgorging, and the bottle is then corked and laid to rest for a short while before it is released from the winery. This is a time-consuming process, and wines produced in this manner are more expensive than those produced by the bulk method.

Charmat Process The bulk process for making sparkling wines. The term *bulk* is appropriate, since in this process the wine undergoes a second fermentation in large tanks. Sediment settles at the base of the tank so that no disgorging (see definition) is necessary. In contrast to the lengthy *champenoise* process described below, the Charmat process takes only a matter of days. This is an inexpensive and quick quick method of producing sparkling wines. Labels must state whether or not the champagne has been processed by the bulk method.

Chillproofing A method of wine clarification. During production, the wine is cooled in order to prevent the cloudiness or sedimentation brought about by extreme temperature changes.

Concord	The dominant grape grown in the eastern part of the U. S., it possesses a distinct taste often referred to as "foxy."
Cooking Wine	Mainly for kitchen use, it contains salt and other spices and often herbs.
Cork Flavor	An unpleasant flavor introduced into the wine from the cork.
Cradle	A receptacle which holds the wine and allows it to rest at a slight angle. It can also be used to assist in pouring the wine.
Crust	A deposit of sediment on the inside of a bottle of old wine. Believe it or not, it is generally a sign of good wine!
Cuvee	A blend of still wines used as a basis for the making of sparkling wines.
Decanting	To pour—usually with a light behind the bottle—from the bottle into another container, observing closely the sediment in the bottle and halting the process when the sediment reaches the top of the neck.
Disgorging	A method for removing the natural sediment in a bottle of sparkling wine, after fermentation in the bottle is terminated.
Earthy	If a flavor of the soil in which the grapes were grown is detected, the wine is said to have an earthy taste.
Enology	The science of wine making.
Fermentation	A chemical process in which the natural sugar and the natural yeast of the grape are transformed into equal parts of carbon dioxide and wine alcohol. Temperature controls are rigidly adhered to during this delicate process.

Fining	The process of clarifying wine. Old-timers used egg white, beef blood or skim milk. Egg white is still used, along with gelatin, bentonite (a clay-like mineral) and casein.
Free-Run Juice	When grapes are crushed in Garolla-type crusher-stemmer machines, the juice which drains readily from the crusher or press without any extra applied pressure is called free-run juice. This is usually fermented separately and produces a superior wine.
Generic Wine	A wine containing numerous grape varietals and usually named after a European wine region (e.g. burgundy, sauterne).
Magnum	A large wine bottle. Usually used for champagne, it holds approximately two-fifths of a gallon.
May Wine	A white wine flavored with the herb woodruff, it is well known throughout Germany.
Must	The crushed pulp and juice of the grape.
Musty Wine	Wine that has developed an unpleasant taste or smell, due to inferior wine making processes, handling or storage.
Noble Mold	A mold which grows on overripe grapes. It rarely appears on California grapes, but in France it is used to produce the best Sauternes.
Oxidation	The chemical reaction that can occur when wine comes into contact with air. Excessive oxidation can ruin a potentially good wine: white wines can take on a brown appearance, and reds can become dulled.

Phylloxera	A root louse which destroyed many vines in Europe and America between 1870 and 1900. A remedy of grafting American rootstocks to European stock proved successful, and the disease was halted.
Racking	The process of removing the clean wine from the tanks, thus leaving the sediment deposit behind.
Tannin	Tannin is an acid which is found in the skins and stems of most fruit. Bitterness can result from excessive tannin in the wine. White wines are generally low in tannin but in reds it can be high enough to induce an astringency. However, tannin can produce desirable flavors if not allowed to dominate the wine's character.
Varietal Wine	A wine named after the grape which accounts for at least 51 percent of its content.
Wine Advisory Board	An organization that assists the California director of agriculture in the promotion of California wines.
Wine Institute	The trade association of the wine growers of California.
Wine Thief	A long glass instrument used by the winemaster to remove a sample of wine from the tank to check its quality.

A Simple Method for Evaluating Wines

The tasting-room host will suggest the appropriate sequence of wines (usually from dry whites through reds to dessert wines). If you have any distinct preferences, however, you should make them known. Remember that some wineries place a limit on the number of wines tasted, and you should take this into account when making your selection.

You will normally be provided with about an ounce of wine in a small glass,

- Hold the glass to the light and study its color and clarity.
- Gently swirl the wine in the glass to expose it to the air; enjoy its fragrance.
- Take a little wine and roll it around in your mouth, savoring its taste and body. If you want an extra little thrill, try the following: cradle a small amount of wine in your mouth while drawing in a stream of air over its surface. This produces a sound somewhat akin to gargling, and is referred to as an "inward whistle." Assuming that you can avoid choking yourself and tolerate the indignant stares of less-informed wine tasters, this simple technique allows you to experience the wine's aroma, through your nose, while enjoying its taste in your mouth.
- Swallow the wine and study its after taste (its cleanness, crispness and overall polish). Bear in mind that you should not feel obligated to drink all the wine. Any unused portion in the glass may be discarded in the receptacles provided in most tasting rooms for that purpose.

VISUAL CHARACTERISTICS (5 points)

Color   Excessively light reds and browning whites are danger signs indicating possible deterioration of quality.

Clarity   California wines generally display a distinct brilliance and are normally free of sediment.

FRAGRANCE CHARACTERISTICS (5 points)

Bouquet   A distinct fragrance originating from the fermentation and aging of the wine.

Aroma   This is the primary fragrance of the grape variety (or varieties) used to produce the wine and can be detected best by using the "inward whistle" technique described previously. Harshness or a vinegary aroma is an indication of a poor wine. Heavy odors of sulfur dioxide or a woody or earthy fragrance detract from maximum scoring.

TASTE CHARACTERISTICS (8 points)

This is perhaps the most important and most complex process of wine evaluation, in which the following factors should be considered:

Tartness   All wines contain varying amounts of sugar and acid. The finest wines contain a perfect balance in relation to their particular characteristics. For example, red wines tend to be dry; but watch out for excess tannin; which can produce a bitter taste. Alternatively, white wines tend to be light-bodied and less astringent than reds, although a lack of acidity or oversweetness is often a sign of a dull wine.

Body   The "weight" of the wine as sensed on the tongue. Again, remember that each wine type (red, rosé, white, etc.) has different sets of characteristics. Most red wines tend to feel heavy, white wines tend to be light.

Grape flavor   The distinctive flavor(s) of the grape or grapes contained in the wine.

GENERAL QUALITY (2 points)

General Quality   Refers to an overall impression resulting from the wine's visual characteristics, fragrance and taste. This is known in wine circles as the "concert." Factors which are considered particularly important are the cleanness, crispness and polish sensed in the aftertaste.

Wine Tasting Log

Date	Winery	Wine Tested	Score	Comments

Date	Winery	Wine Tested	Score	Comments

Date	Winery	Wine Tested	Score	Comments

Date	Winery	Wine Tested	Score	Comments

Date	Winery	Wine Tested	Score	Comments

Date	Winery	Wine Tested	Score	Comments

Date	Winery	Wine Tested	Score	Comments

Date	Winery	Wine Tested	Score	Comments

Date	Winery	Wine Tested	Score	Comments

Wineries by Region

NAPA VALLEY/SOLANO REGION

City	Winery	Page
Calistoga	Sterling	45
Napa	Christian Brothers	28
Oakville	Robert Mondavi	40
Oakville	Oakville	42
Rutherford	Beaulieu	24
Rutherford	Inglenook	32
Rutherford	Souverain	44
St. Helena	Beringer	26
St. Helena	Heitz	30
St. Helena	Kornell	34
St. Helena	Charles Krug	36
St. Helena	Louis M. Martini	38
St. Helena	Sutter Home	46

SONOMA/MENDOCINO REGION

City	Winery	Page
Asti	Italian Swiss Colony	54
Geyserville	Pedroncelli	63
Glen Ellen	Grand Cru	52
Healdsburg	Simi	66
Healdsburg	Windsor	68
Kenwood	Kenwood	56
Rio Nido	Korbel	58
Santa Rosa	Martini & Prati	60
Sonoma	Buena Vista	50
Sonoma	Sebastiani	64
Ukiah	Parducci	62

LIVERMORE VALLEY/EAST BAY REGION

City	Winery	Page
Albany	Bynum	76
Berkeley	Oak Barrel	77
Fairfield	Cadenasso	72

FRESNO/SAN JOAQUIN VALLEY REGION

CUCAMONGA/LOS ANGELES REGION

OTHER WINERIES

NEW TASTING ROOMS

Wineries by Name

FOR AN ENCORE...

If you think we've made some blatant omissions in our winery selections, please send us the name of your favorite spot. If we use it in the next edition, you may win a certificate of merit or an honorable mention. It's worth a try and we'd appreciate it. Just tear out this postcard and drop it in the mail.

Name of Winery _____

Address: _____

Phone No: _____

Wine Tasting Hours: _____

Brief description (list wines, tours, general location, etc.) _____

_____

_____

_____

Other comments: _____

_____

Your name: _____

Your Address: _____

_____

Any comments on the book: _____

_____

CAMARO PUBLISHING COMPANY

P. O. Box 90430

Los Angeles, California 90009

About the Authors

Researching, writing and sketching this book concurrently with *Hidden Restaurants of Northern California* provided an opportunity for Anne and David Yeadon to apply their talents and love for food, cooking, wine and life. Their infectious *joie de vivre* is already well known to California natives and visitors who have sampled their other books, which include *Hidden Restaurants: Southern California* and *Small Towns in California*, the latter in two volumes.

Anne Yeadon is now completing *Towards Independence,* a textbook for teachers of the blind. David Yeadon, who loves to cook, is busy preparing his next gastronomical epic, which will be embellished by more of his delightful sketches.

Other 🅒 *Camaro Guides*

All beautifully illustrated with maps and sketches

. . . For your low cost dining pleasure, plus a few splurges.

- ☐ Hidden Restaurants: Northern California
- ☐ Hidden Restaurants: Southern California
- ☐ Little Restaurants of Los Angeles
- ☐ Little Restaurants of San Francisco
- ☐ Little Restaurants of San Diego

. . . Or for just a bit of adventure throughout the California Countryside.

- ☐ Wine Tasting in California: A Free Weekend
- ☐ L.A. On Foot: A Free Afternoon

TO: Camaro Publishing Co.
P. O. Box 90430
Los Angeles, California 90009

Please send the books checked above. Enclosed is $ _____ which includes $1.95 per book ordered, plus 6% tax and 25¢ postage/handling.

Name _____

Address _____

City _____ State _____ Zip _____

☐ Check here to include your name on the mailing list for new announcements of Camaro's Adventure Guides.

☐ California Wine Tasting Calendar. $3.00 plus tax and 25¢ postage/handling.

California Wine Tasting Calendar with beautiful sketches from Camaro's best selling book, Wine Tasting in California.

(Full size: 22 x 14 inches)

Now Available!

May

Sun.	Mon.	Tues.	Wed.	Thurs.	Fri.	Sat.
			1	2	3	4
5	6	7	8	9	10	11
12	13	14	15	16	17	18
19	20	21	22	23	24	25
26	27	28	29	30	31	

York Mountain Templeton Est. 1889   *Wine tasting 9 to 5 daily*

California Wine Tasting Calendar is available at your bookstore or use coupon at left to order by mail. IDEAL GIFT

Camaro Publishing Co.
Newwest ®

A Special Notice to our readers:

Excellence is our publishing aim—to provide the best, most accurate and timely information in the world about travel/adventure, good food and wine, all at the very lowest prices. We have discovered that you don't have to spend a fortune to enjoy dining out or travel. You just have to know where to go.

To speed making our latest information available to the adventurous, we have just started the **Newwest California Club** which will present monthly, the very latest of the very best. . .and all for not much money. Try it and see.

Newwest California Club Membership

Mail To: Secretary, Newwest California Club
P.O. Box 90430, Los Angeles, Ca., 90009

$3.00 per year or special charter subscription: $6.00 for three years, or $25 for lifetime Gold Circle membership.

Membership includes subscription to NEWWEST.

New Member:

Name_____

Street _____

City, State, Zip _____

Enclosed $ _____.

Hop Kiln Winery

Russian River Valley

1975 Zinfandel

Alcohol 11.5% by Volume

Produced and Bottled by the Hop Kiln Winery, Healdsburg, California

---

Our robust, 100% Zinfandel is made in the classic Tuscan manner of unhurried care, relying on the turn of the seasons to produce a natural wine. Our vineyards, first planted in 1880, are picked at full maturity and the grapes crushed in our landmark Hop Kiln Winery at Sweetwater Springs Historic District.